Building Gold, Silver and Precious Stones

A Devotional Exposition of 1 Corinthians 3:8-15

by

N. A Woychuk, M. A., Th.D.

Cover by Jennifer Lamp

Foreword by

Dr. L. S. Chafer, President of Dallas Theological Seminary at the time.

Foreword to Second Edition by
Dr. T. R. Dunham, Publisher

S M F   P r e s s
P. O. Box 411551 • St. Louis, MO 63141

Building Gold Silver and Precious Stones

ISBN 1-880960-02-8

Library of Congress Catalog Card
Number 00-092718

Printed in the United States of America

Affectionately Dedicated
to
Paul and Marcia Daniels
True and Sincere Friends and Devoted Servants
of our Lord and Savior Jesus Christ

I could not do without Thee, O Jesus, Savior dear!
E'en when my eyes are holden, I know that Thou art near.
How dreary and how lonely this changeful life would be.
Without the sweet communion, the secret rest with Thee!

Contents

Foreword

Since truth respecting the Christian's life and service is so neglected, the message of this book is greatly needed. It should have a place in every Christian's library. Not only is the subject of the volume of vital import, but it is especially attractive because of an unusual gift in writing which the author possesses.

As one who has a lifetime of service behind him, I can say I greatly appreciate the clear and convincing way in which Dr. Woychuk has presented this so important subject.

Until this great theme is fully comprehended, the book will call for repeated readings.

As long as the Lord may tarry and Dr. Woychuk be spared, I anticipate many equally helpful volumes from his pen.

Lewis Sperry Chafer, D. D., Litt. D.
Dallas Theological Seminary
Dallas, Texas   December, 1946

Foreword to Second Edition

It is an honor to have been asked by the author of this *very unusual book* to write a Foreword to this edition, but it is with a feeling of inadequacy to do justice to its worth that I accept the opportunity and undertake the task.

When the manuscript for the first edition came to my hands, I read it with keen and genuine interest, and before I had finished reading, I found myself moved with tremendous emotion to see the truth, the beauty, the faithfulness to certain doctrines of the Word of God, and the illustrations with which these doctrines were adorned and illuminated.

My feeling about the work was that it was the *richest bit of literature* of its particular nature that had ever come across my desk.

The author's work here shows that he is not only conversant with the great truths of "Salvation" and "Rewards," as being distinctly different teachings of the Bible, but he is also true to other fundamental facts relating to these.

In addition to his loyalty to the Faith once for all delivered to the saints, the author shows and teaches the warmth and reality of a definite spiritual walk and fellowship with God, and a devotion to our adorable Lord in a life of service in the things that are foremost in the plan and program of God for the individual believer in this age of grace, when the Holy Spirit is administering God's purposes and work in forming the body of Christ.

The book gives evidence of the author's wide acquaintance with other literature. It contains forceful and useful illustrations, and will move the earnest, honest reader to a closer walk with God, a more faithful work for God, and an increased devotion in the worship of God.

May it please Him, before Whom every believer shall stand at the Judgment Seat, to give the book an ever-widening ministry to the praise of His glory.

T. Richard Dunham, D. D.
Findlay, Ohio   January, 1955

Introduction

While I was still in University a passage of Scripture attracted my attention in a way that has never left me. It is 1 Corinthians 3:11-15:

> *For other foundation can no man lay than that is laid, which is Jesus Christ.*
>
> *Now if any man build upon this foundation gold, silver, precious stones, wood, hay, stubble;*
>
> *Every man's work shall be made manifest: for the day shall declare it, because it shall be revealed by fire; and the fire shall try every man's work of what sort it is.*
>
> *If any man's work abide which he hath built thereupon, he shall receive a reward.*
>
> *If any man's work shall be burned, he shall suffer loss: but he himself shall be saved; yet so as by fire.*

It would seem that building "gold" is intended to suggest the greatest thing that any and every believer could do. But what is building "gold"? The commentaries suggest that it is an imperishable kind of service which would withstand the test of fire. But what is it? What does building "silver" mean? What does building "precious stones" mean?

It is obvious that the Holy Spirit seized upon the standard of the greatest material value—gold—to represent the greatest spiritual value—the greatest thing that any believer may accomplish.

But what is building "gold" then?

What is the greatest service a person can render for God? It is something that withstands the test of fire and is a lasting honor to the Lord.

On September 30, 2000, *Sammie Henson*, age 29, of the St. Louis area, lost the wrestling match at the Olympics in Sydney, Australia. When he was only eight, on a boat on Lake St. Louis, he first declared, "I will be the Olympic champion." He won many wrestling championships, including the 1998 World Championship in Iran. Through the years he worked at it continually, looking forward to the Olympic victory and the *gold* medal. "Gold"—Olympic gold—is what he craved.

When he lost he became totally disoriented and began screaming and wailing like an "animal with its leg caught in a steel trap." His wife and father did all they could but he was inconsolable.

Oh, that as believers we were that eager to gain the "gold" the apostle speaks about to the church at Corinth. Both require discipline. One is achieved by physical effort, the other is gained by spiritual exercise. One receives the applause of the world; the other receives the acclaim of God. One is bound to the standards of earth; the other is tuned to heaven.

Much of what Christians do is only "wood, hay and stubble" and although it may look impressive in the estimation of the world, it cannot stand the test of fire. It perishes, and a lifetime of service is lost.

But before we proceed, let us take a good look at the "foundation": "For other foundation can no man lay than that is laid which is Jesus Christ" (2 Cor. 3:11). God laid the foundation in the work Christ did as mediator between God and men. And no person can build anything upon that foundation until he himself is solidly resting upon that foundation.

Are you trusting Christ as Savior? Are you resting completely upon His finished work in your stead?

The person of Christ and what He actually did for you is the most profound, most positive and most permanent reality than any form of matter or mode of force in existence.

In the next two chapters we will consider our relation to Christ as Savior and in chapter three we will return to take up the subject of what a Christian builds upon that foundation, and what "building gold, silver and precious stones" actually means.

N. A. Woychuk

-1-

The Foundation

Vain are the hopes the sons of men
Upon their works have built:
Their hearts by nature are unclean,
Their actions full of guilt.

Jesus! How glorious is Thy grace
When in Thy name we trust,
Our faith receives a righteousness
That makes the sinner just.

—Isaac Watts

While the bewildered 19th Century was slowly and sadly expiring and remorsefully beating its head against the stone wall because it had contributed so peculiarly toward the spiritual impoverishment of the human race, two men whose feet still stood solidly upon the *Rock of Ages,* were earnestly conversing on this subject as they walked slowly through the woods of England's Hawarden estate. One was an eloquent American preacher; the other was the distinguished Christian statesman and one of England's most honored sons— *Dr. T. Dewitt Talmage* and *Hon. Wm. E. Gladstone.*

"Talk about the questions of the day!" said Gladstone. "There is only one question, and that is how to apply the Gospel to all circumstances and conditions. It can and will correct all that is wrong. I am, after a long and busy life, more than ever confirmed in my faith in Christianity. . . . Dr. Talmage, my only hope for the world is in the bringing of the human mind into contact with the divine revelation."

The starting point in this study is the person of Jesus Christ, who stands solid in the history of men. A real Christ appeared in the world and created the foundations of Christianity. He is the answer to the soul's deepest restlessness and the spirit's profoundest questions. "I am come," He said, "that they might have life and that they might have it more abundantly" (Jn. 10:10).

The person of Christ stands out clear and simple as the powerful Savior of sinful men and women. Paul the Apostle resorted to the strongest words of preface when he would convey the heart of Christ's mission: "This is a faithful saying, and worthy of all acceptation, that Christ Jesus came into the world to save sinners" (1 Tim. 1:15). The force which resides in the person of Christ and His finished work has in itself a purifying, transforming power, a delivering, uplifting, sanctifying power. The gospel of Christ is the gospel of a Person Who saves men from sin and corrects all that is wrong.

"He is such a person as men could not have imagined if they would, and would not have imagined if they could." The one who saw Him face to face, the one who touched His hand and leaned upon His bosom presented with fervent expectation this soul-uplifting, faith-begetting, sin-cancelling wonder of the universe, "And the Word was made flesh, and dwelt among us, (and we beheld His glory, the glory as of the only begotten of the Father,) full of grace and truth" (Jn. 1:14).

Wonder of wonders! Fact so real. Truth so precious. News so exceedingly welcome. The Magna Carta of man's liberation from his greatest enemy. Oh, that everyone had ears to hear and heart to understand the fact more real, more needful, and more life-giving than the breath we breathe—how that "Christ died for our sins according to the Scriptures."

Happy is he who will cast himself upon the foundation which

God has laid. And it is so wonderfully simple: "But as many as received Him, to them gave He power to become the sons of God, even to them that believe on His name" (Jn. 1:12).

A few months ago, while I was visiting in the home of a lovely Christian family growing in grace and in the appreciation of the things of God, the father turned to me as if he had made some startling discovery, "Do you think the people in the church generally understand the meaning of Christ's death in our place?"

If they did, I mused, they would not be so busy and so concerned about "laying again the foundation of repentance from dead works, and of faith toward God" (Heb. 6:1). Or perhaps they are like *Bunyan's* wavering and joyless character Ignorance, who does not doubt the necessity of Christ's atonement, and who seems to *know* the truth, but who is positively *not resting* there for his salvation.

Superstition and ignorance, mixed with those blinding dispositions of self, such as pride and self-sufficiency, in all parts of the world and in all ages, have kept even millions of earnest people from truly seeing the Light of the World. It is this thick darkness that the Holly Spirit must explode before a person will actually rest upon the foundation which God has laid, and be saved from sin.

This thick darkness covers, like a wet blanket, all the heathen religions, and keeps the deluded victims from beholding the invisible God who is clearly seen by the things which are made. It is this same darkness, though lighted by considerable knowledge of God, which basically underlies our much diluted Christianity.

All man-made religion stupidly imagines two false premises. First, that God is against us. Second, that our own painful effort, galling sacrifice, and religious observances will pacify and soften His wrath.

Self-service, and self-sacrifice, mixed with good works, are the foundations of all religions, including the "streamlined unbelief" of the Twentieth Century, which generally but quite inappropriately goes by the name of Christianity today.

Look at that pitiable mother in heathen Africa standing on the bank of the ancient Nile with a baby in her arms, shrieking, moaning, and frothing at the mouth as she dashes that helpless child into the swirling waters: "Now, God, you've got to be good to me! I have given you what is dearer to me than my own life: I have made the supreme sacrifice; you cannot ask anything more." Why, why doesn't someone tell her that Christ "His own self bare our sins in His own body on the tree," and "suffered the just for the unjust that He might bring us to God"?

Look at the Indian Sadhus who afflict themselves with strange vows and practices—binding themselves with chains, running naked in all climates, keeping their eyes closed and sealing themselves in isolated places. What are these "Pharisees of Hinduism" doing? They are zealously seeking personal merit before God. Are they "laying again the foundation of repentance from dead works" because they will not believe that "Christ was once offered to bear the sins of many" (Heb. 9:28)?

Behold the confused nation, Israel, which blindly rejected the Messiah as it continues its "shadows" of animal sacrifices and Mosaic ceremonies. Behold the admixture of Judaism, heathenism, and Christianity in the pompous "masses" of Romanism. Surely these highly "religious" folk heed not the revelation of God which saith explicitly, "Christ being come an high priest of good things to come, by a greater and more perfect tabernacle, not made with hands, that is to say, not of this building; neither by the blood of goats and calves, but by His own blood He entered in once into the holy place, having obtained eternal redemption for us" (Heb. 9:11, 12).

Few, perhaps, in any "Christian" church will actually substitute something they can do *for* Christ, and deliberately say, "I will not be saved by Christ." Many, however, do zealously strive to put something of their own making, Cain-like, *along with*

Christ. It is generally the Bible and Christ; or feelings and Christ; or the Virgin Mary and Christ; or the Church and Christ; or my dead level best and Christ; or prayer and Christ. All these are but subtle forms of unbelief and an evasive form of Christ rejection.

The Gospel of Jesus Christ is designed by the living God to be exclusive. It is utterly and completely exclusive. Notice the *one* Name, the *one* way, and how positively it excludes everything else; as the Holy Spirit slashed away all other foundations, "There is none other Name under heaven given among men, whereby we must be saved" (Acts 4:12), and the word of Christ, "I am the way, the truth, and the life: no man cometh unto the Father, but by me" (John 14:6).

To a little Irish lad in a hospital ward a Christian had given a gospel tract that set forth the way of salvation clearly. The boy had been brought up in the Roman Catholic church and was counting on penances and sacraments to save his soul. But after reading the booklet, light broke in upon his darkened soul, and the next time the visitor came, he exclaimed, as he gave thanks for the message received, "I always knew that Jesus was necessary, but I never before knew that He was enough!"

Search the world over and the ages through; there is no other—either available or efficacious. For soul-salvation there is only one Name. For washing away of sin there is only one sacrifice. For establishing the hope of eternal life there is only one foundation. The essential thing for us, and the exclusive thing for us, is that we stand in living relations of faith to the One whose blood "cleanseth us from all sin."

Many a person has had to see the utter ruin of his buildings *raised on self,* before he could find interest in, or care to build upon the *Rock of Ages.* The real needs of men are common to all men. We all want health, love, knowledge, and truth; and it is equally true that we all desire forgiveness of our transgressions, liberty from the slavery of self and sin, the life of righteousness, and the hope of eternal glory. "Salvation" gathers up all these, and "Salvation is of the Lord." It is passing strange that, like the easy-going, indifferent, materialistic jail-keeper of Philippi, some earthquake, some personal loss, some raging storm, or some blighting chain of circumstances must descend upon us before we will even be shaken down to the "sandy" foundations of our devising and honestly ask the question, "What must I do to be saved?" And even then we still searchingly look upon what *we* might be able to "do," instead of upon that which God has "done."

MAKING THE GREATEST DISCOVERY

A lady, rejoicing in the assurance of her salvation, once said to a man in whose salvation she had been interested for a long time, "Your religion has only two letters in it, and mine has four."

"How's that?" he asked.

You see, he was one of those folk who try to work their own way to heaven by doing good works, attending services, and by carrying out methodically ceremonies and ordinances. The man had never seen himself hopelessly lost and in need of personally and honestly accepting Christ as Savior. He thought he could get there by his own works.

The analysis of the lady puzzled him not a little. "What do you mean," he asked, "by two letter and four?"

"Why, your religion," said the lady, 'is always D-O, DO! Whereas mine is D-O-N-E, DONE!"

This caused him to reflect seriously upon his relation to God. He began to search the Bible diligently. And ere long the Spirit enabled him to see that it was not a matter of what he could do for God, but simply that of accepting as a gift that which God had DONE for him That settled everything for him. He saw the whole truth comprehended in the conclusive words of Ephesians 2:8, 9: "For by grace are ye saved through faith; and that not of yourselves: it is the gift of God. Not of works, lest any man should boast."

> What shall the dying sinner do,
> That seeks relief from all his woe?
> Where shall the guilty conscience find
> Ease for the torment of the mind?
>
> —*Isaac Watts*

While the last drops of His blood were flowing from His bruised body hanging on the cross, He spoke those wonderful words, "It is finished," which have thrilled and burned in many a heart as the light of the glorious gospel of our God broke upon sin-burdened souls. "Christ died for our sins according to the Scriptures" (1 Cor. 15:3). The work for our redemption finished. The foundations for our eternal life laid. Indeed, "good tidings of great joy to all people."

A devout old lady, zealously laboring in the thick darkness of Confucianism to achieve merit before God, sat in the front row listening to a sincere message of the gospel while an American missionary was preaching fervently in her language. Toward the end of the service one night, this Chinese woman shouted out loud, "Chana!" "chana!" which means, "It is finished." Earnestly she continued her confession, "Just think, for all these years I have been reading through thick volumes of stuff and bumping my head (prostrating themselves and bumping the head on the ground as they read those "sacred" thick volumes was supposed to procure for them merit before God), reading and bumping, reading and bumping, and now I see that it is all finished. That sinless Son of God was made sin for me that through it He might make me perfectly righteous in the sight of God."

And then she exclaimed joyfully, "Haja! Haja!" which means, "I believe, I believe."

And thus another soul made the supreme discovery and was gloriously established upon the solid foundation.

"When I was a boy at school," said *Sir James Y. Simpson*

(1811-1870), M. D., of Edinburgh, Scotland, "I saw a sight I can never forget—a man tied to a cart and dragged before the people's eyes through the streets of my native town, his back torn and bleeding from the lash. It was a shameful punishment. For many offences? No, for one offence. Did any of the townsmen offer to divide the lashes with him? No; he who committed the offence bore the penalty alone. It was the penalty of a changing human law, for it was the last instance of its infliction.

"When I was a student at the University, I saw another sight I can never forget—a man brought out to die. His arms were pinioned, his face was already pale as death—thousands of eager eyes were on him as he came up from the jail in sight. Did any man ask to die in his place? Did any friend come out and loose the rope, and say, 'Put it around my neck, I die instead'? No; he underwent the sentence of the law. For many offences? No; for one offence. He had stolen a money parcel from a stagecoach. He broke the law at one point, and died for it. It was the penalty of a changing human law in this case also; it was the last instance of capital punishment being inflicted for that offence.

"I saw another sight I shall never forget—myself a sinner, standing on the brink of ruin, condemned to eternal punishment in the lake of fire. For one sin? No; for many, many* sins committed against the unchanging law of God. I looked again, and behold Jesus Christ became my Substitute. He bore in His own body on the tree all the punishment for my sin. He died on the cross that I might live in the glory. He suffered, the JUST for the unjust, that He might bring me to God. He redeemed me from the curse of the law. I sinned and was condemned to eternal punishment; He bore the punishment and I am free. The law of God required a perfect righteousness which I never had. Again I looked unto HIM and found that Christ is the end of the law for righteousness to every one that believeth. The law required spotless purity and I was defiled with sin. Again I looked unto HIM who loved us and

*The author, however, believes the one dark, damning sin is the rejection of Christ Jesus, as Savior.

washed us from our sins in HIS own blood. I was a child of Satan, a child of wrath, but as many as received HIM to them gave HE power to become sons of God, even to them that believe on HIS name. And I found in HIM not only my Substitute, but the full supply of every need of my life.

"I long to tell you of the Savior, 'for there is none other Name under heaven given among men whereby we must be saved.' "

And when Sir Simpson, this world-famous doctor, who discovered the use of chloroform in surgery, was asked what was the greatest discovery of all that he had made, he promptly replied, "That I was a great sinner, and that Christ is a great Saviour."

It is this "greatest discovery of all," as Simpson called it, which he and millions of others, great and small, through the ages have made, and have proven the Gospel of the Lord Jesus Christ to be completely solid and substantial and satisfying—this "greatest discovery of all" still finds the vast multitudes of Satan deluded and self-blinded folk utterly unresponsive to its claims and advantages.

When the astronomer *Galileo* (1564-1642), discovered that the earth moved around the sun, he was laughed to scorn, and the authorities of the Romish Church even threatened the astronomer with the stake if he did not recant his opinion. But now, every child in the schools is taught that the earth goes round the sun.

When the great surgeon *Harvey* (1578-1657), discovered the circulation of the blood from the heart to the extremities, he was ridiculed and disbelieved on every hand. But now, when you are stricken with fever, the first thing the doctor does when he enters the room is to lay his finger on your pulse, and that way he finds the sure indication of the disease. No doubts now that the blood circulates.

When the engineer *Watt* (1736-1819) discovered that steam was a mighty force, the world was skeptical as to its practicality. And when *Stephenson* (1741-1848) constructed his locomotive and utilized the power of steam, he was sneered at as being visionary. But now every express roaring through the country at the rate of a mile a minute is their triumphant vindication.

When *Morse* (1791-1872) discovered that electricity could be transmitted through a wire, and a message could be flashed across the oceans in the fraction of a second, people were sure this was talking of impossibilities. But it is in constant use today.

All the remarkable discoveries and the advantages which they bring to man in the physical aspect of life are universally accepted and heeded, and he who still scorns them is just as universally labeled "a fool." But the "greatest discovery of all" still finds a world careless and indifferent to its claims.

Must you be told again that you are a sinner? Must you be told again that Christ died for your sins? And if you do know this, even if you know nothing else that is revealed in God's Book, you are scholar enough to be saved. "Christ came into the world to save sinners."

What will it take to cause you to see and understand and rest upon that which God has done for you? Listen and heed and live! "Wherefore also it is contained in the Scripture, Behold, I lay in Sion a chief corner stone, elect, precious: and he that believeth on Him shall not be confounded" (1 Peter 2:6).

God sent not His Son into the world to condemn the world, but in Him to provide a ransom for sin-doomed, hell-bent humanity, so that the world through Him might be saved.

Christ was *tried* by temptation and other suffering, and so proved able and sufficient for the work of salvation. As the lamb before her shearers is dumb, so He opened not His mouth, but bore in His own eternal self the torments and suffering of hell and became the "Lamb of God, which taketh away the sin of the world."

THE SURE FOUNDATION LAID

"The Lord hath laid on Him the iniquity of us all" (Isa. 53:6). Since God is absolutely just, He must punish every sin. But God is far from being "against us," or desiring our subjection and torment in hell. Nay, far from it. The opposite is the eternal fact. "God was in Christ, reconciling the world unto Himself" (2 Cor. 5:19). He could not ignore the righteous demands of His own holy person. He could not overlook sin. The solution came in His inscrutable plan and purpose through the death of Christ in our stead. On the cross of Christ all our sins were settled for. Christ endured in our stead the penalty our sin deserved. Christ made an atonement for our sin. That is the reason that God can now save sinners who receive Christ and be righteous in doing so.

The searching Greek scholar, *Socrates* (470-399 B. C.),who raised more questions than he answered, several hundred years before Christ, was perplexed as to how a righteous and just God could possibly save sinful people. He said querulously, "It may be that the Deity can forgive sins, but I do not see how." If Socrates had lived to see Christ die on the cross, or had he "condescended" to read and believe the word of revelation through Isaiah, even as summarily recorded in Chapter 53:5, 6, he could have understood how a righteous God can save sinners and be just in doing so.

Christ was wounded, bruised, chastised, and crucified in our stead. Some people say they cannot understand this. A skeptic once told the famous scientist, *Sir Isaac Newton* (1642-1727), "I do not see the atonement in the Scriptures." "Sir," replied Newton, "sometimes in my absent-mindedness I try to light my candle with the extinguisher on. You take the extinguisher off, and you will see the atonement."

J. Pierpont Morgan (1837-1913), probably the greatest financier this world has ever known, shows in the opening paragraph of his will what appears to be an intelligent appreciation of the substitutionary work of Christ. Here it is, lest you did not notice it in the papers: "I commit my soul into the hands of my Savior, in full confidence that, having redeemed it and washed it in His most precious blood, He will present it faultless before the throne of my Heavenly Father, and I entreat my children to maintain and defend at all hazard and any cost of personal sacrifice the blessed doctrine of complete atonement for sin through the blood of Jesus Christ once offered, and through that alone."

Turn away from your own efforts, your ceremony, your church, your kindnesses, your resolutions, your sacrifices, and see what God has *done* for you. Earlier today a friend of mine said, "It must be very difficult for a Roman Catholic to become converted." It is. But, as a matter of honest fact, it is just about as difficult for a nominal Protestant, who knows all *about* Christ, but who never did honest business with God in accepting Christ as Savior, to be "born again" of the Spirit of God.

Consider for a moment this one verse. From it two great lights flash forth—one upon *God*, and one upon *ourselves*: "For He hath made Him to be sin for us, who knew no sin; that we might be made the righteousness of God in Him" (2 Cor. 5: 21).

Here is the light upon *God*! For it is the triune God who does it all: "He hath made Him to be sin for us." When we see Christ identifying Himself with our sinful race and going up to the hill Golgotha to become the permanent sacrifice for sin, we know that the heart of God is thus entangled in the pain and sorrow, and the hands of God are stretched out to save us from sin (2 Cor. 5:18, 19). That is why this message is so subduing, so morally magnificent. It was of the message of this verse that the greatest German poet, *Goethe* (1749-1832), said, "There is nothing Diviner than this."

Now here is the light upon *ourselves*! "That we might become the righteousness of God in Him." We thus become clothed with the righteousness of God. We become as righteous as Christ in the sight of God.

The converted Chinese quaintly relates how he first made that "greatest discovery of all" and was saved: "I was lying in a deep, dark pit, with no hope of rescue, and ready to die. Confucius came by, and looking in, said, 'If you ever get out, be careful not to get in again.' Next, a Buddhist priest came by, looked in, and said, 'Poor fellow, I am very much pained to see you there; if you only come up part of the way, I might help you.' At last there came one called Jesus, and His face was bright with kindness. He came right down into the pit where I lay helpless, lifted me clear out of it, washed away my uncleanness, clothed me in white raiment, and said, 'Go, and sin no more.' "

Christianity has an organization. Christianity has a doctrine. Christianity has ordinances. Christianity used weak vessels as channels. But the "force" of Christianity is the person of Christ in His death and resurrection.

His universal invitation is, "Come unto me, all ye that labor and are heavy laden, and I will give you rest" (Matt. 11:28).

Here is a good summary of Christ's completed work: "And I, if I be lifted up from the earth, will draw all men unto me" (John 12:32).

We shall, perhaps, never fully understand the meaning of that sublime transaction upon Calvary, but we know experientially now that its relation to the human heart is luminous and life-begetting. It does take away sin. Kneeling at that holy place, the trusting soul at once remembers most vividly, confesses most humbly, and loses most entirely all its guilt. A sense of profound, unutterable relief, sacred quietude, and joy diffuses itself through all the recesses of the troubled spirit. Looking unto the crucified, risen Christ, we receive an assurance of sins forgiven, which goes deeper than man's thought can fathom, and much deeper than his words can measure.

In the New Testament, in the Acts and Epistles, and in the

history of the believers down through the vista of centuries, we see the operation of the mighty Gospel, whose abiding source is Jesus Christ the Lord. It was this force that sent the Apostles out into the world, reluctantly at first, then joyfully and triumphantly, like men driven by an irresistible impulse. It was the revelation of Christ as Savior that converted them, the love of Christ that constrained them, the power of Christ that sustained them. He was abidingly their certainty, their strength, their peace, and their hope. For Him they labored and suffered. In Christ they glorified, and for His sake they lived and died.

A sure foundation! God has done it. God has spoken. He has caused His voice to be heard in this dark, sinful world. It is as though our gracious God had said to us, "Here, I have begun on the new. I have laid a foundation. I have established the ground of redemption, which nothing can ever touch, neither sin, nor Satan, nor death, nor life, nor angels, nor principalities, nor powers, nor things present, nor things to come, nor height, nor depth, nor any other creature, including even your own self. Indeed, nothing shall be able to separate you from the love of God which is in Christ Jesus our Lord, (Rom. 8:38, 39). I *lay* the foundation and pledge My word that whosoever believes; whosoever commits himself in childlike, unquestioning confidence to My Foundation; whosoever rests in My Christ; whosoever is satisfied with My precious, tried, chief Cornerstone shall never—no, never—no, never be disappointed, never be put to shame, never be confounded, 'shall never come into condemnation, but is passed from death unto life.' "

-2-

Established Upon the Foundation

Triumphant Faith!
Here is a conquering path to Heaven,
With feet fire-shod, because her hand is placed
Immovably in God's: her ye doth rest
Unchangeably on His.
—*Miss Tatham*

Did not our hearts burn within us as we gazed upon that *precious* and *sure* foundation which God has laid in the Lord Jesus Christ!

"And he that believeth on Him shall not be confounded," but shall be eternally and securely and comfortably hidden in that mighty "Rock of Ages."

You may be established upon that Foundation, and the Lord Jesus Christ become your Savior from sin upon *one* condition, but that condition is inexorable: it is *faith*—simple, unquestioning trust in the Lord Jesus Christ as the complete sacrifice for your sin. This is the one sole, but indispensable means of being *mortised* upon the foundation which God has laid for our salvation.

Nothing will ever be right until you get on this ground. You have looked upon that Foundation. You have seen what God has done for you. Now cease from all your doings, cease from your own reasonings, cease from your own feelings, cease from your own restlessness, and repose in full, unquestioning confidence in the one offering of Jesus Christ, which has perfectly satisfied and glorified God as to the great problem of your sin and guilt. "This is the work of God, that ye believe on Him whom He hath sent" (John 6:29). This is the only means by which the sacrifice of Christ can benefit you and make you a recipient of the unsearchable riches of Christ.

Christ fills the heart and pervades the life of all who trust Him personally and definitely. A living faith always lays hold on the living God. Faith in Christ is never repulsed; it is never disappointed; it always works. This is because the living God will always answer faith, and thereby fulfill His rich and precious promises to usward who believe. The living God delights in faith. He delights to be fully counted upon. The deeper the need, the darker the surroundings of gloom, the more He is pleased with that grasp of faith which draws upon Him and His immutable promises.

Nothing can ever lift you up from the miry clay of sin and establish your feet upon the Rock, Christ Jesus, except a personal faith in a living personal Savior—God. Faith is the only thing that brings God into the situation and connects you with His infinite resources. Faith makes you owner of all Christ's infinite worth.

What Is Faith?

The one thing that shows whether or not your faith is of the right quality is the *object* of your faith. There is no other test. There need be no fears beyond that. Make certain only that Jesus Christ as your sin offering is the one object of your faith.

Remember the story of the bewildered lady in the inquiry room? The personal worker was saying to her, "Believe; believe; can't you believe?" She kept replying in seeming agony, "I canna, I canna." Then another worker came up and said, "Mother, can't you believe *Him?*" She promptly answered, "Oh, yes! I can believe *Him!*" That changed her thought from *faith* to the *object* of faith. Never think or be concerned about your faith, but think about Christ.

Stand still before God and let this burn into your soul. The *object* of faith, therefore, is not the Bible, but the Christ of whom the Bible speaks; not the creed, but the Christ of whom the creed is true; not the cross, but the Christ who died on it for your sin. You need not sigh about your small faith or be concerned about your inability to exercise the living faith. You need only to look upon your changeless Mediator.

You may not know how the Spirit moved to convince you of sin, reveal Jesus through the Word, and create faith in Him. You will probably never understand how this saving faith to you He did impart, or how, by believing in His Word, peace was wrought in your heart. But this you know, and in this you may even now rejoice: "I know *whom* I have believed, and am persuaded that He is able to keep that which I have committed unto Him against that day" (2 Tim. 1:12).

Those are words full of comforting truth and insight with which the deeply spiritual English preacher, *F. B. Meyer* (1847-1929), pled earnestly with an audience at the great Northfield Bible Conferences, as he sought to point out that faith, never so small, if directed to the person of the Lord Jesus Christ as Savior, was sufficient to tap the power of God for salvation. He said, "If your faith be infinitesimal, if it be full of changeful emotion, if it be groping in the dark, if it be unable to see closely the face of Christ, if for long months you have not the conscious enjoyment of Christ; yet, if your faith is reaching out its trembling hand toward Christ, that movement proves your faith to be the faith that binds you to Christ, and you are the child of God."

Faith is but the stretching out of the hand to grasp His extended hand. The Savior cannot hold you up nor give you the blessings of which His hands are full, if you keep your hands listless by your sides or resolutely clinched behind your back. Faith is the opening of the heart for the inflow of His gifts. The sunshine cannot enter the house when doors are barred and windows shut. Faith is but the channel through which His grace pours, but it is obvious that it cannot enter if there be no channel. Faith is the flight of the soul toward Christ—the soul that realizes its danger and flees to its hiding place.

President Mark Hopkins once said, "Faith is believing that God will do as He has promised." And *Dr. Horace Bushnell* defined it as follows: "Faith is not a mysterious possession; it is a simple act. Faith is that act by which one person, a sinner, commits himself to another person, a Savior." Faith simply takes God at His Word, undisturbed and undeterred by what may be seen without or felt within. "For by grace are ye saved *through faith;* and that not of yourselves: it is the gift of God: not of works, lest any man should boast" (Eph. 2:8, 9).

Established By Faith

Wonderful Savior! All His preciousness, all His power, and all His divine prerogatives are made available for the believers in the infinite grace of God. Through faith in Christ we are "made perfect." Through faith in Christ we are "stablished" upon the "foundation." Through faith in Christ we are "strengthened" with might in the inner man. Through faith in Christ we are "settled" in unmoved repose upon the Rock of Ages. Cleansing from sin, deliverance from Satan's bondage, fixity of character and purpose, strength for service or for suffering, all these come to us from union with Christ, the foundation.

Our organic oneness with Him is not only like the resting of a building on a rock, it is like the rooting of a tree in the ground from which it draws nourishment; and more wonderful still, it is like the union of a branch with the stem from which it draws life. If we rest by faith on Jesus Christ, we have the ground for assurance of sins forgiven, and a foundation on which we can build holy and blessed lives. Then if we but keep near to Christ, His life will freely flow through ours and make us that we shall neither be barren nor unfruitful in the knowledge of our Lord Jesus Christ.

You may feel weak and broken and soiled and helpless, and your faith may be no larger than the smallest seed, a grain of mustard seed. Yet, if your faith is resting in the Lord Jesus Christ as Savior, there will surely come the new life, born of the spirit, and the sure hope of life eternal.

Look at that tiny grain of seed (your simple faith), way down in its little grave in the ground. Spring comes. There is a gentle knock at the lacerated exterior of the tiny seed. It is the knock of "Mother Nature," which is God. She says, "May I come in?" And the seed, from within, cries out helplessly, "I have nothing to give you. I am broken, helpless, torn, and at the end of myself." But "Mother Nature" asks again, "May I come in?" And the seed replies this time with arms of receptivity, "You may if you will."

The door flings open and "Mother Nature" pours a tiny, trickling stream of her powerful energy into the perforated, bruised, broken mustard seed; and the pulse of life is felt within, forcing down the rootlet into the soil, and forcing up a spire, which makes its way through the heavy clay that conceals it, until at last the little green shoot raises its tiny head above the surface of the ground, looks around, and exclaims joyfully as if from an impact of a great discovery, "Perhaps I can after all; if 'Mother Nature' goes on pouring her wonderful energy into me, there isn't much that I can't do." So the root goes deeper, and the spire grows higher, and thus the plant develops and becomes full grown. It is not just the seed; it is "Mother Nature" in the seed.

Strictly speaking, the analogy is not entirely satisfactory, because the new life of a believer is wholly from without, from above, and there is no vitality in an unsaved human being that would respond in spiritual growth when exposed to the proper conditions. The seed has life latent in it which responds to certain conditions and produces life. Human beings are totally dead, and utterly without any innate spiritual life, even in embryonic form. It must be entirely of God. We reach out by simple faith, and by the Holy Spirit the seed of the new life is planted within, and through the efficacy and life-giving power of Christ's death and resurrection, we are made new creatures after His likeness. Thus we see that it is all of Him.

It is no longer the fussy, active, restless running around hither and thither, doing this, and doing that, and doing the other. You have ceased from your own profitless doings, which are but as "filthy rags" in the sight of God. You are resting by faith in a divinely accomplished work. "To him that *worketh not*, but believeth on Him that justifieth the ungodly, his faith is counted for righteousness" (Rom. 4:5).

Let me here suggest just this one word of explanation that might help you to follow on through with these thoughts. When you receive Christ as Savior by faith, you are instantly and permanently saved from sin's *penalty*. This does not mean that you become perfect *experientially*, nor that you will not be tempted again to sin, and even unwillingly to falter in sin. Indeed, it is a daily warfare, and you can only be saved from the *power* of sin each hour as you reckon and rely upon your Friend and Savior. And, finally, you will be completely saved from sin's power and even from sin's *presence* when you are called Home to God, and your body is also made new.

You have trusted Christ for salvation; you are also trusting Him daily for deliverance from sin's power. God is now working in you to will and to do of His good pleasure, and you are working out all the good works that God is working in you according to the energizing of the Holy Spirit. You can never actually serve Christ until you know and believe how He has served you. You can never give God anything until you have first of all received at His gracious hand His "unspeakable gift." You cannot have a stream without the fountain.

"Not by works of righteousness which we have done, but according to His mercy He saved us, by the washing of regeneration, and renewing of the Holy Ghost" (Ti. 3:5). By regeneration we understand the commencement of the life of God wrought in the soul of man through faith in Jesus Christ. Please observe that it is *not* "the regeneration of washing" (as those who would insist that this refers to water baptism would make it read), but "the washing of regeneration." It speaks of the cleansing that is effected in us by the washing of the Holy Spirit on the ground of the shed blood of Jesus Christ. This marks the beginning of the new life, which had not an existence before. The "renewing of the Holy Ghost" speaks of the invigoration of that which has been begun, the sustenation of a life already possessed. And so we see it again: Saved by grace through faith, and sustained and strengthened by the Holy Spirit.

FAITH ANALYZED AND COMPARED

Indeed, there is positively no other way by which we may receive the "cup of salvation" except by the hand of faith.

"Therefore, being justified by faith, we have peace with God through our Lord Jesus Christ" (Rom. 5:1). The first word, "therefore," refers to the helplessness of man, and also the marvelous provision which God has made for our salvation, as shown in chapters three and four of Romans. "Being justified" means being cleared of every charge of guilt and so forever free from judgment. How is this accomplished for us? "By faith"—which shuts out all thought of works, and points solely to the one simple act in which one person, a sinner, commits himself to another person, the Savior. "We have"—here and now, a present assurance, not merely a vague future hope. "Peace with God"—all strangeness and alienation and condemnation in the sight of God is gone, and the conscience is purged from the guilt of sin; in God's presence we are in perfect peace, reconciled and raised to the position of sons, "to the praise of the glory of His grace, wherein He hath made us accepted in the Beloved."

Look at Romans 10:9, 10, where the words of promise in

golden letters shine. "That if thou shalt confess with thy mouth the Lord Jesus, and shalt believe in thine heart that God hath raised Him from the dead, thou shalt be saved. For with the heart man believeth unto righteousness; and with the mouth confession is made unto salvation." Two things seem to be the condition here, at first sight, instead of one: "Believe in thine heart," and "confess with thy mouth." Let's examine them.

"Believe in thine heart." Salvation is for those who believe. It is for the heart. Sin has smitten us with heart disease; God, in His mercy, has provided the heart cure. If the remedy is to touch the disease, it must be received in the heart. You can readily understand that this business of "believing in the Lord Jesus Christ as personal Savior" is not at all synonymous with casually "believing in God" (this the devils do and tremble, the Scripture says); it is not mere knowledge *about* Christ and His death; it is not just a mental assent. It is facing the issue of sin, and believing on Christ "in the heart." A Chinese convert said, "I came first with my eyes, then with my ears, then with my heart." No doubt, first she *saw* some believers, then *heard* the Word of God and the voice of God, and then *believed* on Christ in the heart.

"Confess with thy mouth." This is *not* another condition of salvation. Strictly speaking, it is an integral part of "believing in the heart"; *it is but an outward expression of an inward reality.* Just as truly as there is a stream where there is a spring; so there must be confession where there is faith. Confession is faith uttering itself. Confession is just faith turned from its obverse side to its reverse. This interrelation of faith and confession is excellently explained by *James Morison* (1816-1893): "When faith comes from its silence to announce itself, and to proclaim the glory and the grace of the Lord, its voice is *confession.*"

A similar two-fold view of saving faith is suggested by Acts 20:21—"repentance toward God, and faith toward our Lord Jesus Christ." In the original, Luke uses but one article with the two nouns (Taen metanoian kai pistin), indicating that repentance and faith constitute a unit idea, and that either noun involves the other; either might be used alone to convey the same thought. "Repentance" emphasizes, perhaps, more pointedly the issue of sin which must be faced and reckoned with when a person is reconciled to God through faith in the Lord Jesus Christ. But let it be forthwith remembered that there never is any such thing as saving faith—the eager flight of a soul to its precious Hiding Place—without clear recognition of sin's penalty and power and honest reckoning therewith. A lost soul, sinking dangerously in the quicksands of sin, certainly does face the issue of sin when it reaches out its trembling hand of faith to the gracious and mighty arm of the Savior.

Then there is that clarifying word of John 1:12, 13: "But as many as received Him, to them gave He power to become the sons of God, even to them that believe on His name: Which were born, not of blood, nor of the will of the flesh, nor of the will of man, but of God."

"As many as received Him": This is only another form of the expression at the end of that verse, "believe on His name." To receive Christ is to accept Him with a willing heart, and to take Him as your own Savior. It is but another form of expression for that justifying faith which unites the sinner's soul to Christ. As someone has said, "To believe on Christ with the heart is to receive Him, and to receive Him is to believe on Him."

"To them gave He power to become the sons of God": This expression means, "He gave them the privilege of adoption into God's family." The word "power" means "right or privilege." It does *not* mean strength or ability. It does *not* mean that Christ confers on those who receive Him a spiritual and moral strength, by which they convert themselves, change their own hearts, and make themselves God's children. The Greek word translated "power" is used 102 times in the New Testament, "and never," as *Bishop J. C. Ryle* (1816-1900), points out, "on one occasion in the sense of physical, moral, or spiritual strength to do a thing.

It is generally translated 'authority, right, power, liberty, jurisdiction.' "

"To them that believe on His name": The word "name" is put for the person, who is the object of saving faith. Believing on Christ's name is that faith of reliance on Christ as our Savior, and is that faith which reaches out to receive salvation and justification from the gracious hand of God.

"Which were born": The birth here spoken of is that "new birth," or regeneration, which effects a new life in a person through the Holy Spirit at the time that person receives Christ. A person thus born of God is "a new creature: old things are passed away; behold, all things are become new" (2 Cor. 5:17).

"Not of blood, nor of the will of the flesh, nor of the will of man, but of God": Believers do not become what they are "by blood," that is, by blood connection with godly ancestors. Salvation does not descend from parent to child. Nor do believers become "new creatures" by the "will of the flesh,"—that is, by the efforts and exertions of their own natural hearts. Nature is never able to change itself. "That which is born of the flesh is flesh." Nor do believers become God's children by the "will of man"—that is by the acts and deeds of ordained ministers, priests, or anyone else. Man cannot regenerate hearts. "But of God"—a person becomes saved and regenerated and new solely and entirely by the grace of God. The new birth comes through the converting, renewing, and sanctifying grace of God in the heart of the person that truly "receives" Christ as Savior. They are "born of the Spirit."

Saving faith and regeneration are inseparable. The new birth is not a change that takes place *after* a person has believed in Christ. The very moment that a man really, with the heart, believes in Christ, however feebly, he is "born of God." The weakness of this faith may not make him immediately conscious of the transaction, just as a newly-born infant knows practically nothing about itself; but where there is faith in Christ, there is always the new birth, and the person can wholeheartedly know that he is saved, and confidently rejoice in the assurance of his salvation: I KNOW THAT I AM SAVED FROM SIN'S PEN-ALTY, FROM ITS JUDGMENT, AND THAT I AM GOING TO HEAVEN.

Resting Upon the Foundation

A lady once said to *Mr. D. L. Moody* (1837-1899), "I think it is presumption to say 'I am saved.' " To which Mr. Moody firmly and quite accurately replied, "It is presumption on your part to say that you are not saved when God says you are." Indeed, indeed!

The living God of the Bible, Creator of heaven and earth—this God has laid for our salvation a sure and precious foundation. He has said in numerous places that you are saved forever the moment you receive Christ. We have been considering a number of Scripture passages of what "saith the Lord" on this matter. Listen to this: "There is therefore now no condemnation to them which are in Christ Jesus" (Rom. 8:1). And again, "These things have I written unto you that believe on the name of the Son of God; that ye may *know* that ye have eternal life, and that ye may believe on the Name of the Son of God." (1 Jn. 5:13)). And yet again, "Verily, verily, I say unto you, he that heareth My Word, and believeth on Him that sent Me, hath everlasting life, and shall not come into condemnation; but is passed from death unto life" (Jn. 5:24).

It is presumption and stubbornness and foolhardiness on your part to say that you are not saved when God says you are. Now are you? Have you admitted honestly before God that you are utterly lost in sin, and helpless yourself to do anything about it? Have you reached simply but earnestly and honestly to the Lord Jesus Christ in faith and received Him into your heart as Savior? Have you made that "greatest discovery of all" and acted on it?

Many folk seem to stumble on that word "believe." They say invariably, "Why, I have always believed." Just a minute now. From early childhood you have believed *in* the living God, known much *about* Christ's life and death, but you have *not always* believed in the Lord Jesus Christ as your own personal Savior from sin's penalty. There is a vast difference. Just as much difference as there is between knowing a certain banker, knowing all *about* him, and even knowing him personally and doing some business with him; and that further and definite experience when you found yourself bankrupt and went to him and asked him specifically to pay you out.

John G. Paton (1824-1907), famous missionary to the New Hebrides, wanted to translate the gospel according to St. John into the native language. He worked on it a while and then it appeared he could make no further progress. He could not find out what the word for "believe" was in the native tongue. "Believe" is the key word in John's gospel, and occurs there some ninety times. So, reluctantly, he laid aside his manuscript.

One day a native worker returned from service over the hills, and he sat down in one chair and stretched out both legs on another chair in Paton's office, and as he did so he used a native word, which means "I am resting my whole weight" on these chairs.

Paton jumped up with rejoicing and said "I have my word." He translated the gospel of John, and every time he needed a word for "believe," he put in the native word which means "resting my whole weight upon."

Try it and see how it works! The earnest inquirer asked the Apostle Paul, "What must I do to be saved?" And the answer was, *"Rest your whole weight* upon the Lord Jesus Christ, and thou shalt be saved, and thy house"* (Acts 16:30, 31).

It does make sense. It is absolutely true. It always works. It is so simple that a young child can understand it and act on it, but it is also as profound as the heart of God. Do not despise its simplicity. It is not cheap. It cost a price so great that its value cannot on earth be fully appreciated nor computed.

Dr. G. Campbell Morgan (1863-1945), whom God used so extensively on both sides of the Atlantic in preaching the gospel, relates an interesting experience: "Some years ago in Yorkshire, England, I had been speaking of God's utter forgiveness, and a miner said to me in an after meeting,

" 'Mr. Morgan, it is altogether too cheap. I would like to believe it, but I can't believe if I merely turn to Him that immediately God will forgive me.'

"I looked at him and I said, 'My friend, have you been at work today?'

" 'Yea,' he answered, 'I have been in the mine.'

" 'And how did you get home? You were four hundred yards under the earth; how did you get up?'

" 'I got up as I always do,' he said; 'I stepped into the cage at the bottom of the shaft, and I was pulled up, and I came home.'

" 'How much did you pay to come up?'

" 'Pay!' he said, 'I paid nothing.'

" 'Don't you think it was too cheap?'

" 'Oh, but,' he said, 'it is very different. It cost the company a lot of money to sink the shaft, though I paid nothing.'

"That is it, that's the Gospel."

> "Nothing in my hand I bring,
> Simply to Thy cross I cling."

ASSURANCE OF SALVATION

It cost God everything to sink the shaft in laying that foundation, which is Jesus Christ. It costs you nothing to rest your whole weight upon it, but He will lift you up. "For Christ also hath once suffered for sins, the just for the unjust, that He might bring us to God" (1 Pet. 3:18). When you receive Christ, you literally stand "where the fire" of God's wrath has already burned:

> I come, Lord, in penitence, sorrow and shame,
> I come, my Redeemer, Thy pardon to claim,
> I come, Lord, I come in Thy Wonderful Name,
> I stand where the fire has been.

The fire of God's wrath burnt Him in my stead,
My Lord, and my Savior, who suffered and bled,
The whole of my guilt on His innocent head:
    I stand where the fire has been.

I stand, Lord, and worship in gratitude sweet,
I stand, and in reverence I bow at His feet,
I stand, Holy Father, in Jesus complete,
    I stand where the fire has been.
             —*A. F. H.*

Faith enables us to rise to the highest heights of expectation and rejoicing, even as Peter did in that all-comprehensive, all-wonderful passage, 1 Peter 1:3-8. Peter knew he was saved. He was certain of his inheritance in heaven. He was confident that he would be kept through the power of God. He rejoiced in his salvation, even amidst heavy testing. He sincerely loved the blessed Lord. And thrice blessed are they who have not seen Him, but have believed on Him and love Him and rejoice in Him.

"He that believeth on Him shall not be confounded." "Unto you therefore which believe He is precious: but unto them which be disobedient, the stone which the builders disallowed, the same is made the head of the corner, and a stone of stumbling, and a rock of offence, even to them which stumble at the word, being disobedient" (1 Pet. 2:6-8). Do not forget that grim alternative. Do not let the very simplicity of the gospel become to you a stumbling stone and a rock of offence. The freeness and simplicity of the gospel of salvation by faith has necessarily a dark underside, and the more clearly and joyfully the one is proclaimed, the more clearly and solemnly should the other be emphasized.

What is it that causes this Christ to become a stumbling stone and the rock of offence? Notice again in that passage above how significantly "disobedience" is made the antithesis of "believing." Disobedience is unbelief. It is an act of the rebel will. It is a rejection of Christ. If you are not saved today, it is not just because of your sin, but, basically, it is because you have rejected the Savior who died for your sin. May this fact haunt you and follow you and hotly pursue you until you humbly fall at the Savior's feet and make Him your own. Remember that you do not have to do anything to reject Christ. Just go on as you are, even attempting and succeeding in doing your dead level best. Just remain in unbelief. Just neglect receiving the Savior.

Unbelief, like some malignant alchemy, perverts all Christ's preciousness to harm and loss, as some plants elaborate poison in their tissues from sunshine and sweet dews. There will surely come to us from Him either the gracious influences which save, or the terrible ones which destroy. He is either the merciful Fire which cleanses and transforms, or the awful fire which consumes. Faith builds on Him as the Foundation, and makes the soul forever secure. Unbelief pulls down that Rock of Ages on its own head as the rock of offence, and is ground to powder by the fall.

Queen Victoria, of England, attended a service in St. Paul's Cathedral and listened to a sermon which caused her to ask her chaplain, "Can one be absolutely sure in this life of eternal safety?" The poor chaplain, himself blind, endeavoring blindly to lead the blind, gave her the answer that he "knew of no way one could be absolutely sure."

This was published in the *Court News* and read by a humble minister, *John Townsend*, who was a great friend of *George Muller*. After much thought and prayer, Mr. Townsend sent the following note to the Queen:

"To Her Gracious Majesty, our beloved Queen Victoria, from one of her most humble subjects:

"With trembling hands, but heart-filled love, and because I know that we can be absolutely sure even now of our eternal life in the Home that Jesus went to prepare, may I ask your Most Gracious Majesty to read the following passages of Scripture: John 3:16; Romans 10:9, 10.

"These passages prove there is full assurance of salvation by faith in our Lord Jesus Christ for those who believe and accept His finished work.

"I sign myself, your servant for Jesus' sake,"

"John Townsend."

Much prayer from many hearts went up to God concerning the result of this letter. In about two weeks a modest-looking little envelope was received:

"To John Townsend:

"Your letter of recent date received, and in reply would state that I have carefully and prayerfully read the portions of Scripture referred to. I believe in the finished work of Christ for me, and trust by God's grace to meet you in that Home of which He said, 'I go to prepare a place for you.' "

"Signed,

Victoria Guelph"

May the Lord be pleased through His own Word to reveal to you the "sure foundation," to enable you to take the simple step of faith which establishes you upon it, and to fill your heart with the assurance of your salvation forever.

Forces without will threaten your peace; forces within will test your confidence in the Lord.

But, amidst all circumstances, may you react as did Judah's king, Jehoshaphat, when surrounded by an overpowering alliance of enemy nations. Jehoshaphat looked diligently to the Lord God of heaven, took fresh stock of the everlasting promises of God which forever guaranteed God's covenant with His chosen people, and then poured out his child-like confidence into the ear of God: "O our God, wilt Thou not judge them? For we have no might against this great company that cometh against us; neither know we what to do: *but our eyes are upon Thee*" (2 Chron. 20:12).

God wonderfully came to his rescue: "Be not afraid nor dismayed by reason of this great multitude; for the battle is not yours, but God's . . . Stand ye still, and see the salvation of the Lord with you" (2 Chron. 20:15, 17). The deliverance came, and all Judah praised God. Jehoshaphat rose up to counsel the people. Notice it carefully—it is for you also: "Believe in the Lord your God, so shall ye be established. . . . Praise the beauty of holiness. . . . Praise the Lord; for His mercy endureth for ever" (2 Chron. 20:20, 21).

—3—

Building Gold

"I would converse with Thee from day to day,
With heart intent on what Thou has to say,
And through my pilgrim walk, what'er befall,
Consult with Thee, O Lord! about it all.
Since Thou art willing thus to condescend
To be my intimate, familiar friend,
Oh! let me to the great occasion rise,
And count Thy friendship life's most glorious prize!"

Now, what does building "gold" mean?

You are saved. You are God's child. You are going to heaven. You are yet on the earth.

"Now if any man build upon this foundation gold, silver, precious stones, wood, hay, stubble; every man's work shall be made manifest: for the day shall declare it, because it shall be revealed by fire; and the fire shall try every man's work of what sort it is" (1Cor. 3:12, 13).

Once saved—resting securely upon that foundation—as God's child you can build upon this foundation *selfishly*—"wood, hay, stubble"; or build upon it *for the glory of God*—"gold, silver, precious stones."

Gold! Gold! Gold! "If any man build upon this foundation—gold. . . ." Gold comes first. It is intended to suggest the *greatest thing* that a Christian can do. It describes a work most abiding, a service of highest rank.

What is building "gold"? What is the greatest thing that you or any other believer, irrespective of ability, position, age or means, can do for God today?

Is it preaching the gospel to large throngs? Nay, for a person may preach to others with tongues of angels and golden oratory, yet himself be as sounding brass or a tinkling cymbal, disapproved of God. Is building gold contributing generously to provide for the needy, sending missionaries abroad, or building elaborate cathedrals? Hardly so. A person may give all his goods to feed the poor, contribute large sums to the church budget, and erect magnificent buildings, yet himself not even be established upon the foundation.

Not everything that glitters is gold! Gold is considered nonperishable. Gold belongs to the aristocracy of the hills and is the king of metals and minerals. Gold is the most costly.

Although gold coinage was unknown in the early Old Testament times, it was, nevertheless, regarded as the symbol of earthly riches (Job 22:24) and was used as the most convenient way of treasuring wealth. A common practice was to make gold into jewelry with the dual purpose of luxurious adorning and the treasuring of the metal.

Gold was the highest standard of values (Prov. 3:14); hence, it was most worthy for the description of the adornment of angels (Rev.15:6) and saints (Psa. 45:13), and for the preparation of the sanctuary and furnishings in the worship of God. In the long list of offerings ordered to be brought by the children of Israel for the purpose of erecting the Tabernacle, "gold" is listed first (Ex. 25: 1-8).

The idea and arrangement of the Tabernacle was to make

for sinful men an approach to a holy God, creating privileges, dignities, and responsibilities of drawing nigh to the Divine Presence and enjoying the worship and communion there. God said, "Make me a sanctuary; that I may dwell among them" (Ex. 25:8).

In the construction of this Tabernacle, noteworthy is the fact that the boards round about were overlaid with gold, and that the Ark with the Mercy Seat, the Table of Shewbread, and the Candlestick—these three outstanding furnishings depicting the presence of the Triune God—were fashioned and adorned with pure gold. This precious metal was thus used at the divine command to burnish the sanctuary whereof God said, "I will *commune* with thee from above the mercy seat" (Ex. 25:22).

It is interesting to note how this *communion with the Living God* above the mercy seat was made resplendent with earth's most precious metal—gold.

"Now if any man build upon this foundation gold . . ." In order to portray the greatest thing a person, redeemed by Christ's precious blood, can do for God, the Spirit-directed writer couches the truth in one single word, "gold." The standard of the greatest material riches is seized upon as a symbol for the greatest spiritual values. What then is building "gold"?

CONSCIOUS COMMUNION WITH GOD

I submit that "Building gold" *is conscious communion with God*—a child of God in vital, direct, and personal fellowship with the heavenly Father. "And truly our fellowship is with the Father, and with His Son Jesus Christ" (1 Jn. 1:3).

The greatest thing you can do for God today is simply to commune intimately with Him. This may sound strange at first thought. We might be inclined to consider time so spent as indolence and waste, "mere loitering about God's throne," as I heard a prominent Texas statesman once describe it. Indeed, people, yea, Christians, seem exceedingly slow to recognize its true worth. Just like when the Mount Morgan Gold

Mine in Australia was first opened up, some half a century or more ago, a poor farmer sold the land, which he had dexterously tilled for years, to the Morgan Brothers for $3,200 and went insane, sometime after, when he found that the same land was sold for forty million dollars. All about him was the "king of metals," rightly his, if only he had discovered and mined it, but he entered not into the possession of its value.

Just as naturally, just as easily, and just as tragically—only with longer and more serious consequences—do most Christians who are busy "cultivating" for God miss the unsearchable riches of God, by failing to mine the "gold." Time spent with God is time spent most profitably. Such soul rest refreshes all life's energies, redeems the time, and is the sure minister of progress. The hour of seclusion with God never fails to enrich the public service. The men and women who richly adorned their earthly pilgrimage with good works, whose much fruit abides, and whose influence lingers with heavenly fragrance like some royal oriental perfumes—these crowned saints earnestly urge upon us the incomparable value of "building gold."

There is *Samuel Rutherford* (1600-1661), of Anwoth, of whom it is said, "He was always praying, always preaching, always visiting the sick, always catechizing, always writing and studying." This fair little man of Puritan days who showed to many the "loveliness of Christ," says to us, "Ye must, I say, wait upon Him, and be often communing with Him, whose lips are as lilies, dropping sweet-smelling myrrh, and by the moving thereof He will assuage your grief; for the Christ that saveth you is a speaking Christ; the church knoweth Him by His voice (Song 2:8), and can discern His tongue amongst a thousand . . . . This is the earnest which He giveth sometimes, and which maketh glad the heart: Peace of conscience, liberty of prayer, the doors of God's treasure cast up to the soul, and a clear sight of Himself looking out and saying, with a smiling countenance, *'Welcome to Me, afflicted soul.'* "

Robert McCheyne (1813-1843), of Dundee,Scotland, whose life was a passionate abandon to the love of Christ, and who died when but thirty years of age, reckoned communion with God highest on his daily list: "I ought to spend the best hours of the day in communion with God. It is my noblest and most fruitful employment and is not to be thrust into any corner."

And a refreshing word from the beloved *Andrew Murray* (1828-1917), who has taught so many the value of "abiding in Christ": "Let every approach to God and every request for fellowship with Him be accompanied by a new, definite, and entire surrender to Him to work in you. . . . As you tarry before God, let it be in a deep, quiet faith in Him, the Invisible One who is so near, so holy, so mighty, so loving. Let this be also a deep, restful faith, a confidence that all the blessings and powers of heavenly life are around you and in you. . . . Begin each day thus in fellowship with God, and God will be all in all to you."

And the blind poet, *Milton* (1608-1674), looked deeply into these things when he said, "They also serve who only stand and wait."

Mind, soul, and spirit engaged with the person of God in quiet meditation and consultation is the fountain of all God-honoring service. From it rises all other fruitage. It is a basic essential. Without it, all other activity is mere dross and din. In the blessed bond of fellowship with God all our spiritual resources are found, and His strength is there perfected in our weakness; therein are the fruits of the Spirit mellowed and ripened, and believers made to conform to the Savior's likeness.

"What man is he that desireth life, and loveth many days, that he may see good?" (Psa. 34:12). Does not this place before you that full, abundant life to which you have secretly aspired—"a large life, a life of spacious activities, of grand persistence and continuity"? That the blessedness of this spacious life with its divine flavors and essences may be yours is clearly indicated by the significant context in which this question is raised by the Psalmist. If we compare this blessed life to a plant, we may see in the preceding verse 9 the tap root through which the nutriment for this life rises; it is this: "O fear the Lord, ye His saints: for there is no want to them that fear Him." We note that this root reaches away into union with God.

On the other hand, following the Psalmist's analysis of the blessed life, we have in verse 13 the spire and fruitage of the plant: "Keep thy tongue from evil, and thy lips from speaking guile." This takes up the truth of our relationship with those about us and pure fellowship with other believers. This shall be the subject of our thoughts in the succeeding chapter.

Let us turn back to the root of this blessed life: "O fear the Lord." This is not synonymous with terror; rather, it suggests the thought of deep reverence, perception, and sensitiveness. The "fear of the Lord" is that delicateness before the Lord which enables the soul, exposed before Him like a sensitive plate, to discern His most silent approaches. This explains well the meaning of that familiar word, "the fear of the Lord is the beginning of wisdom."

Just as sensitiveness in music is the beginning of musical advancement, and the sensitiveness in art is the beginning of competence in that field, soul sensitiveness toward God is the beginning of wider discernment in the knowledge of God and fuller efficiency in the doing of His holy will. This is the fountain of the blessed life, and there is "no want to them that fear him." "To thrill to His faintest breathings, to hear the still, small voice, to catch the first dim light of new revelations, to be exquisitely responsive to the movements of the Father," as *Jowett* (1864-1923) says, "is to sink deeply the tap root for a full and spacious and fruitful life." It brings delight to the heavenly Father's heart. It enables Him to reveal His gracious heart more adequately to us who are the objects of His fondest affection.

Robert Browning (1812-1889), poetically tells the story of Andrea del Sarto, a famous painter in Florence. In his youth, del Sarto married a woman of rare beauty. She was, however, a shallow-minded, superficial creature. She was the woman, who, with a careless swing of her skirt, smeared the noble picture he had painted in hours of great spiritual ecstasy. She filled his life with disappointment. Not because she robbed his hand of its deftness, or his mind of its genius, or his soul of its inspiration—the tragedy was this: she was heart-blind: she never understood the moral majesty of his mind; she never genuinely entered into the great spiritual hunger of his heart. Consequently, he could not disclose to her his noblest and his best self. Even so, the yearning God is able to reveal Himself to us only in proportion to our soul capacity and sensitiveness.

Oh, that your love might indeed "abound yet more and more in knowledge and in all judgment; that ye may approve things that are excellent" (Phil. 1:9, 10), and that ye "may be able to comprehend with all saints what is the breadth, and length, and depth, and height; and to know the love of Christ, which passeth knowledge, that ye might be filled with all the fulness of God" (Eph. 3:18, 19).

Sonship depends upon faith; fellowship, upon conduct. There can be no fellowship with God apart from implicit obedience of His Word, and joyful submission to His will. It is possible to be a Christian and yet not have fellowship with the Father. God is essentially, changelessly, undisturbedly, eternally holy. He is the Light, or, as the Psalmist said, "He covered Himself with light as with a garment." There is, therefore, no such thing as having fellowship with Him and walking in darkness, for walking in darkness is sin. "If we say that we have fellowship with Him, and walk in darkness, we lie, and do not the truth: but if we walk in the light, as He is in the light, we have fellowship one with another, and the blood of Jesus Christ His Son cleanseth us from all sin" (1 Jn. 1:6, 7).

This does not mean that we attain here the state of perfection. We do not. The passage quoted above suggests a progressive sanctification and cleansing. It is in the present tense. But the main direction of our lives should be toward the light—seeking by aspiration, by deliberate choice, by conscious effort to live a life holy and acceptable unto God. Thus we shall continuously be delivered from the power of sin, and have fellowship with the Father.

When did you last have real fellowship with God? Please understand the question. *When were you definitely occupied with God and enjoying His presence?* Is not your fretting, your fussing, your fuming, your fainting evidence enough that you have long time been absent from Hebron. Now, "Hebron," a city of Judah, twenty-two miles south of Jerusalem, means "fellowship." After receiving its meaningful name in Joshua's time, Hebron became one of the favorite camping places of the Patriarchs, where they resorted for fellowship with God. When the land was finally conquered, Caleb, the man who dared to believe God in the face of tremendous opposition, stepped forth and claimed Hebron for his *permanent* possession. He was not content simply to visit there now and then. Caleb *lived* at the place called "fellowship," and there he built much "gold." Oh, that "Hebron" were *our* constant abiding place.

The world of doubt and unbelief creates a refrigerating process on our zeal and enthusiasm in things of God. The shocks of the daily grind, the distractions of the unbelieving world tend to push back the invisible realities into the dim background and seriously drain our spiritual strength. Even in the service of Christ, the constant going and coming externalizes our life, draws our interest to the outside of things, and submerges the spiritual realities. We become more interested in the organization than the holy purposes which it was designed to advance. It makes us feverish about the transient and negligent of the eternal.

What Christian has not felt himself weary in body, mind, and soul as a result of these draining seductions, and, with the contemplative *Wordsworth* tempted to cry out,

> The world is too much with us: late and soon,
> Getting and spending, we lay waste our powers.
> Little we see in nature that is ours:
> We have given our souls away, a sordid boon.

Divorced from companionship with God by the glitter of

this world, we become like the one who, engrossed in fireworks, forgot the glory of the stars. He had been busy enlarging his barns, and neglecting the need of his thirsting soul. Neither hot nor cold, he becomes distasteful to God, who exclaims, "I will spue thee out of my mouth." Depressive, worryful, unattractive to those about him, he persists in that dark, morbid spirit, muttering to him, "I am rich, and increased with goods, and have need of nothing." And the Spirit of God records forthwith concerning such, "And knowest not that thou art wretched, and miserable, and poor, and blind and naked" (Rev. 3:15-17).

Christians? Yes, but far removed from Hebron—out of vital contact with God. We need the calming, cooling, sanctifying presence of the Lord! The still small voice of God follows the distracted sons, with sympathetic solicitude, endeavoring to win them back to His inner circle: "I counsel thee to buy of me gold tried in the fire..." (Rev. 3:18). How loving the Spirit of the Father. Not threatening, not rebuking, but tenderly beseeching, "I *counsel* thee." And the counsel is "to buy gold tried in fire."

This is God's advice, again, to build "gold." Communion with God is here singled out as being the lukewarm believer's chief need. But more still, it is to be "gold tried in fire." God is not unmindful of how subtly the world in many ways pulls on the believer who would walk close to the Lord. Therefore, fellowship with God, under circumstances geared up in every way to distract and disturb and deter, is, indeed, "gold tried in fire."

Our possession of God is made possible through faith, and faith is, by no means, encouraged through contacts with the world. Furthermore, delighting in a God, whom we see not, is contrary to this world's operating principle of sight. God is the Christian's living hope, "wherein ye greatly rejoice, though now for a season, if need be, ye are in heaviness through manifold temptations: that the trial of your faith, being much more precious than gold that perisheth, though it be tried with fire, might be found unto praise and honour and glory at the appearing of Jesus Christ: whom having not seen, ye love; in whom, though now ye see Him not, yet believing, ye rejoice with joy unspeakable and full of glory" (1 Pet. 1:6-8).

Buffeted, bewildered, and beset with bitterness of mind and soul, still the trusting child of God nestles to his Father's side, desiring none other in heaven or earth. This is gold tried in fire. As bees gather their honey from flowers in all sorts of different and uncongenial places, oftentimes, and store it in the honey-comb, so the man of God garners from all circumstances of life, even those most adverse, and through communion with his Father, transmutes the gathered substance into abiding spiritual meat and drink.

"As the hart panteth after the water brooks, so panteth my soul after thee, O God. My soul thirsteth for God, for the living God: when shall I come and appear before God?" (Psa. 42:1, 2). The nearer we are to God, the more fully we are satisfied with Him rather than with His gifts. We delight to hear His gentle voice, "soft as the breath of even, that checks each thought, that calms each fear, and speaks to us of heaven."

> Once it was the blessing,
>   Now it is the Lord;
> Once it was the feeling,
>   Now it is His Word;
> Once His gifts I wanted,
>   Now the Giver own;
> Once I sought for healing,
>   Now Himself alone.
>
> —*A. B. Simpson*

Enjoying God's Presence

A wise leader in the devotional life has said that if we have but three minutes for prayer, two should be spent in realizing and enjoying God's presence. He with whom our hearts are enraptured is in truth our God. All too frequently we give the Lord God of heaven but an empty profession, tolerating with passive endurance some formal service and then running home or elsewhere to enjoy to the full that home-made god, whatever it might be. *Martin Luther* said, "Whatever thy heart clings to and relies on, that is properly thy god." To the god which we enjoy we confide and whisper, "In thy presence is fulness of joy." Our true living God is grieved, and our own thirsting souls are shriveled every time we allow ourselves to be occupied with any home-made god in preference to Jehovah.

Like marching music, those age-old words—stimulating, noble, and eternal—summon the heart of earnest manhood: "Man's chief end is to glorify God and to enjoy Him for-ever." To glorify God is to enjoy Him. That was the spirit of the first Christians, who "did eat their meat with gladness and singleness of heart, praising God." John, in love with the Lord, was a happier man than the mighty Herod in all his pretensions. St. Peter had more solid joy in one hour with an angel, God's messenger, by his side, than Nero did in all his tu-multuous career strumming his fiddle to appease his rapa-cious gods.

> Oh, the pure delight of a single hour
> That before Thy throne I spend,
> When I kneel in prayer, and with Thee, My God,
> I commune as friend with friend.
>
> —*Fanny J. Crosby*

As we draw nigh to God in blessed communion, we may well imagine Him saying to us, as someone has suggested in part:

"My child, it is not necessary to know much about Me. It is sufficient to love much. Speak to Me as thou wouldst to thy mother.

"Are there any for whom thou wouldst pray to Me? Re-peat to me their names; after each name add what thou wouldst have Me to do for each of them.

"Are there graces thou wouldst ask for thyself? Write the long list of all the needs of thy soul, and come and read it to Me.

"Tell me simply how proud thou are, how sensitive, how egotistical, mean, and indolent. Poor child, do not blush; there are in Heaven many saints who had thy faults, which little by little were corrected.

"Do not hesitate to ask Me for blessings for the body and mind; for health, memory, success. I can give all things, and do give always blessings needed to make your soul more holy.

"Hast thou plans to occupy thee today? Lay them all before Me, and I will give thee strength to do everything well and profitably.

"Hast thou no zealous thought for Me? Dost thou not wish to do a little good to the soul of thy friend who perhaps has forgotten Me?

"Hast thou not troubles? Who caused thee anguish and pain? Bring to Me all your failures, and I will show thee the cause of them. Tell me all, and I will bless.

"Hast thou not joys to make known to Me? Why dost thou not let me share thy happiness? Tell me what has happened since yesterday to cheer and console thee? An unexpected visit which did thee good; a success thought impossible; a fear suddenly removed; a mark of affection; a letter; a gift which thou hast received? I prepared it all for thee.

"And that continual temptation! Are you resolved not to expose yourself to it again, and refuse to answer its demands? Hast thou refused kindly to fellowship with that companion who leads thee into sin? I will give you strength to do it, if you will.

"Well, my child, go now; I enjoyed being with you; take up thy work; be silent; be humble; be submissive. Come back soon and bring me a heart still more devout and loving. Tomorrow I shall have more blessings for thee."

God's heart, longing with infinite love, desires to enjoy the trophies of His grace.

Sadhu Sundar Singh effectively illustrates this thought for us: A mother once hid herself in a garden of densely growing shrubs, leaving her little son alone, surrounded by the trees, plants, flowers, vines, grass and fountains, enchanting with aroma and beauty. The little fellow searched through the whole garden, but he could not find her.

The gardener said to him, "Sonny, don't cry! Look at the mangoes on this tree." But the child persisted, "I want my mother."

He picked up the lad in his arms, carried him to a beautiful bed of flowers, pulled one, and holding it up to the boy's face, he said, "Doesn't it smell wonderful?" "No! No! I want my mother," came the words from his broken heart.

Again the anxious servant tried. He led the boy to the fountain and tried to attract his attention to the refreshing spray falling gently on the green grass and shrubs round about. But with nothing would the child be comforted, crying out louder and louder, "I want my mother! The food she gives me is nicer than all the mangoes, her love is sweeter than all these flowers, and her presence is more satisfying than all these fountains and springs, and indeed, you know that all this garden is mine, for all that my mother has is mine. No! I want my mother."

When the mother, hidden in the bushes, heard this, she rushed out, and pressing her child to her breast, she covered him with kisses, and right then that garden became a paradise to the child.

Does not the Lord walk in the midst of His children, seeking them and calling them each one by name in this great garden of a world? How shall He find us—absorbed with these things, or crying out, "Whom have I in heaven but Thee? and there is none upon earth that I desire beside Thee. . . . One thing have I desired of the Lord, that will I seek after; that I may dwell in the house of the Lord all the days of my life, to behold the beauty of the Lord, and to inquire in His temple" (Psa. 73:25; 27:4). We should feel the pull "nearer to God" as did the saintly *Faber*:

> God loves to be longed for, He loves to be sought;
> For He sought us Himself, with such longing and love;

He died for desire of us, marvelous thought;
And He yearns for us now to be with Him above.

HIDDEN MANNA

In His presence alone is fulness of joy, and at His right hand there are pleasures forevermore. All others are broken cisterns, wells without water. Every human idol eventually totters and falls. Nothing else can satisfy our craving for that highest fellowship.

What sober gaiety there is in the Lord. What solid joy. How hearty and infectious the merriment! Everything will give us a lift if we are in close communion with our God. If the heart is attune with Him, we will verily hear the angels crying one to another, "Holy, Holy, Holy, is the Lord of hosts: the fulness of the whole earth is His glory." In all our ways we shall go out with joy, we shall be led forth with peace, the mountains and hills shall break forth before us into singing, and the trees of the field shall clap their hands!

The beneficent sun shall be to us as His smile. All nature shall reveal His handiwork shouting in our ears: "God!" "God!" "God!" The flowers will blend their hues, joining chorus with the birds to the praise of our blessed God. For many hours one night I listened to the mocking bird imitating some twenty-three bird calls, and in each one I thought I could detect some expression of praise, of adoration, of communion with God, such as "Rejoice evermore!" "Trusting Him!" "Bless Him!" "Praise Him!" "God!" "God!" "God"

The birds of the air so exuberantly triumphant and satisfied, so laughingly defiant in their security, stirred afresh my longing after God. These words were clamoring for utterance: "O magnify the Lord with me, and let us exalt His name together" (Psa. 34:3). Then I rested on these words, "To him that overcometh will I give to eat of the hidden manna, and will give him a white stone, and in the stone a new name written, which no man knoweth saving he that receiveth it" (Rev. 2:17).

"A new name," "the white stone," and "the hidden manna"; these are the victor's life-secret. The "new name" is one of endearment from the Father. The "white stone" suggests some enlargement of capacity, personality, character. Then what is the "hidden manna"? It surely refers to those hidden resources, that strengthening and sustaining food given them whose delight is in the Lord.

"Hidden Manna!" This is that heavenly sustenance that Christ referred to when upon the earth He said to His disciples, "I have meat to eat that ye know not of." And like many Christians today, the disciples could not understand that; they said, "Hath any man brought Him ought to eat?" Then the Lord, who communed with the Father unceasingly, replied, "My meat is to do the will of Him that sent me" (Jn. 4:32-34). This secret food is most nourishing. That princely preacher, *J. H. Jowett*, spoke solid truth when he said, "There is more real recreation in one hour of communion with Christ, that in a whole week of social revelries, however gracious and worthy they may be."

To partake of this "hidden manna" we must have daily that sacred "silent time." A thousand things there are which tend to vex our spirits, break our calm, and exhaust our supply of grace. Manifold temptations there are which would make "lean" our life with artificialness, formality, worldliness, and frivolity. As we pass amidst such dissipating, secularizing influences, we need desperately to be "silent unto God," and feast upon the "hidden manna," and learn over and over again that God remaineth faithful despite all changeful circumstances.

The moon in the sky is shining with full, silvery brightness, while a man is gazing upon its perfect reflection down in a deep, still well, and remarks to a friendly bystander, "How beautifully fair and round she is tonight! How quietly and majestically she rides along!" Just then the friend dropped a pebble into the well, which causes him to exclaim, "Why, the moon is all broken to shivers, and the fragments are shaking together in awful disorder."

"What gross absurdity! Look up, man! The moon has not changed one jot or tittle; it is the condition of the well which reflects her that has changed."

Your own heart is the well. When there are no disturbing elements allowed therein, the Holy Spirit takes the preciousness of Christ and reveals it to you for your comfort and peace. But the moment a wrong motive is cherished in the heart, the well is seriously disturbed, and your glorious experiences are smashed to pieces, and you are restless and disturbed within.

But look up! "He abideth faithful! He cannot deny Himself!" Be still before God, confess that sin, and instantly there will be restored once more the calm sweet joy of communion.

"My soul, wait thou only upon God; for my expectation is from Him. He only is my rock and my salvation: He is my defence; I shall not be moved" (Psa. 62:5, 6). We must rouse our souls to contemplation of God—"My soul!" "Wait thou only upon God," or, as the Revised Version has it, "Be thou silent unto God." Linger before God in composure, in tranquility, in chastened silence. God's people are to be a quiet people, dwelling in the heights of purity, and softness, and therein remain utterly unruffled. As the smooth surface of the well best reflected the beauty of the moon, so in the believer the reflection of Christ is clearest where the life is most calm.

Do not feel that you have to entertain God. Just be silent unto God. Rest in the Lord. Repose with confidence upon His bosom, and the peace of God which passeth all understanding shall overflow your tired soul. You shall then exclaim, "My *expectation* is from Him!" The word "expectation," we are told, might be translated "line" or "cord." Though our circumstances vary, still that "cord" binds us to the Lord. I stood at the lake shore at camp one night when the moon was out in full brightness. Stretching across the calm waters, there was a golden "line" between me and the moon. I walked along the shore, and the golden "cord" upon the water moved with me, but remained unbroken. This, I thought, is, indeed, my "line," my connection with God. "My *expectation* is from Him." It shall never be broken. And I could almost hear His reassuring voice across the waters, "My presence shall go with thee, and I will give thee rest" (Ex. 33:14).

Rudyard Kipling (1865-1936), faintly whispered something on his sick bed. The nurse inquired, "I beg your pardon, Mr. Kipling; I thought you wanted something." "I do," faintly replied the sick man; "I want my heavenly Father. He only can care for me now." In his extremity the distinguished writer found comfort and peace and security only in the presence of God, and experienced the "cord" of His promises binding him strongly to the sure Rock.

The life of nature tends inevitably downward: your eyes will grow dim, your natural force will be abated, your body will become a burden, your years will be changed from buoyancy to dreariness, and you shall "utterly fall." All this is brought out by Isaiah in 40:30. Do not stop there, though. Notice the next verse. "But they that wait upon the Lord shall renew their strength; they shall mount up with wings as eagles; they shall run, and not be weary; and they shall walk, and not faint." This suggests the possibility of immortal strength, inexhaustible because of constant replenishment.

That word "wait" implies the thought of taking time with God, delighting to be with Him, and profiting by such familiar contact, even to the extent of conforming to His likeness.

There was once a painter who had three scholars. They seemed all anxious to learn the secret of their master's power. The first spent all his time in the studio at his easel. He copied incessantly the master's great pictures, looking deeply into their beauties, and trying to imitate them with his own brush. He was up early, and last to leave the workroom at night. He had nothing to do with the master himself, attended not his lectures, and did not associate with him in conversation and questions. This scholar lived and died, and never expressed on canvas a single one of the noble characteristics of his master.

The second scholar, on the contrary, spent little time in the studio, scarcely saw his palette, or wore out a brush. He attended every lecture on art, was constantly asking questions about theories of perspective, coloring, light and shade, grouping of figures, and all that, and was a zealous student of books. But for all his study he died without producing a single worthy picture to delight mankind and perpetuate his master's glory.

The third was as careful in the practical work of the artist as the first, and as zealous in the theoretical as the second, but he did one thing which they never thought of doing—he came to know and love the master. They were much together, the young artist and the older one; and they had long talks about all the phases of an artist's life and work. So close and continual, in fact, was their communion that they grew to talk alike, and think alike, and even, some said, to look alike. It was not long before they began to paint alike, and on the canvas of the younger glowed the same beauty and the same majesty that shone from the canvas of his master.

REPLENISHED FROM ABOVE

The parable is not hard to interpret. If we "delight" in Him, we shall be replenished from above.

Such communion not only glorifies the Father; it is most enriching to us. "Delight thyself also in the Lord; and He shall give thee the desires of thine heart" (Psa. 37:4).

Is there with you a lack of material and physical things—food, clothing, shelter, health? *Delight thyself in the Lord!* "But my God shall supply all your need according to His riches in glory by Christ Jesus" (Phil. 4:19). He shall fill your cup to overflowing. He shall prepare a table before you full of good things. He shall lead you beside still waters and satisfy you in green pastures, and you "shall not want."

Do you feel depressed with disappointment and peculiar heaviness of heart? *"Delight thyself in the Lord!"* He will "cleanse the stuffed bosom of that perilous stuff which weighs upon the heart." God will restore your soul and renew a right spirit within you.

George Friedrich Handel, (1685-1759), sat in his London office in 1741, ill in body, bankrupt financially and spiritually, apparently all through as a musician. In the wise providence of God, a certain *Dr. Jennens* sent Handel a compilation of prophecies concerning the descent and ministry of Christ, and suggested that Handel work them up into an oratorio. For twenty-four days Handel was withdrawn from the things of the world, often as not, the food which his man-servant brought to him was left untouched. In the process of working out the great "Hallelujah Chorus" the heart of Handel was melted in adoration of God, and the servant found the musician a new man, with tears streaming from his eyes. Afterward Handel explained, "I did think I did see all heaven before me, and the great God Himself."

He saw God and communed with Him, his power, his perspective were restored. His cold heart was melted and purified as he was received up into glory and caught a glimpse of God. It is no wonder that from its creation until the present the "Hallelujah Chorus" in the Messiah on every rendition transports the hearers heavenward and causes them, as King George III said, "to see the stars shining."

Do you sigh for cleansing and for a quickened zeal in the Lord's work? *"Delight thyself in the Lord!"* He will create in you a clean heart, and renew a right spirit within you. He will wash you thoroughly and cleanse you from your sin. He will restore unto you the joy of your salvation (Psa. 51:10-12).

Isaiah was confused and heavy-hearted and heard not the bidding of God. After the transforming vision of "the Lord sitting upon a throne, high and lifted up," and the subsequent pressing of the live coal on the lips to take away iniquity and purge all sin, Isaiah "heard the voice of the Lord" and found himself quite spontaneously willing and ready: "Here am I, send me" (Isa. 6:1-8).

Oh, remember, friend, that neither joy, nor peace, nor fruitfulness comes from within or from without us; it is rather the result of our union and communion with God. As *Oswald Chambers* (1874-1917) put it, "The Christian worker is one who perpetually looks in the face of God and then goes forth to talk to people." And the painter *da Vinci* (1452-1519), observed, "When I pause the longest, I make the most telling strokes with my brush."

Are the springs of true appreciation and gratitude in your heart choked up, and do you lack perspective and power? *"Delight thyself in the Lord!"* The genial springs will flow again. The eyes of your spiritual understanding will be opened, and you will once again be enthralled with the beauty of the Lord.

On our way up to Winnipeg, Canada, some years ago, we drove by way of scenic Colorado. For years I had been anxious to see for myself "sunrise from Pike's Peak." In Colorado Springs I inquired about it. "Yes, you can go up," they said, "but you will have to get up at 2:00 A. M. and the fare will be five dollars."

We arose at 2:00 A. M. Higher and higher we climbed until the peak was reached, not without dizziness and "fear tremors." Anxiously we waited in the crisp freezing temperature. Slowly dawn's rosy steps were advancing on the eastern sky, until the few broken clouds, hanging above the horizon as if purposefully for effect, were gloriously lighted up into a fuchia red against a background of brilliant blue. And then "Old Sol" tipped the horizon and presently came forth ablaze with divine glory, adorned as "a bridegroom coming out of his chamber."

Standing there on an elevation almost three miles above sea level, we scanned the horizon some one hundred twenty-five miles away and actually looked *down* upon the sun. I gazed upon this beauty with an indescribable inner exhilaration, as if under the spell of some strange magic. My mind, soul, and spirit feasted sumptuously. The vision inflamed my imagination and became a permanent part of my life, just as much as if some special "tabernacle" had been built to preserve it. It became a thing of beauty whose loveliness increases, and it shall never pass into nothingness. We descended the mountain. We continued our journey north. The vision lingered.

We passed through the lonesome rolling country of Wyoming, the unexpected marvels of the Black Hills, the rich fertility of the Dakotas and Manitoba. Then Winnipeg, and the thrill of returning to the city of boyhood days, and seeing again the old familiar flag waving high. Lake Winnipeg, in its ocean-like vastness, was more impressive than ever. We went out to Western Ontario, and I was delighted with the romantic Lake of the Woods and its thousands of idyllic islands. But in all these wonderful sights, the magnificent vision of sunrise from Pike's Peak retained a strange preeminence and gave me a peculiar sense of values and meaning and appreciation for all the rest.

Dear friend, look "full into His wonderful face," gaze and feast upon His beauty, and lo, the vision glorious will endow all the rest in your life with meaning, and will sanctify for your good even the simple and familiar things of life. *"Delight thyself in the Lord."* He will unstop the springs of your life. He will become your highest and your best perspective.

Or is it general doubt, uncertainty of the future, and fear of the enemy that is hindering your sojourn in the narrow way and is dimming your vision of the Celestial City? Then, again I say, *"Delight thyself in the Lord!"* He shall promptly dispatch the heavenly footman, goodness and mercy, to your succor, and they shall follow you all the days of your life until the house of the Lord you reach.

Go yonder with Bunyan's pilgrim up that Hill Difficulty, and for refreshment stop with him in the Palace Beautiful. The King's daughters, Prudence, Charity, and Piety, will discourse with you on the sufferings of Christ in our behalf and the glory

that shall surely follow. You will retire for the night in a large
upper chamber, with windows open toward the Sunrising. There
you will rest in body, mind, and spirit, and you will awake with
the sun, singing with Bunyan,

> Where am I now? Is this the love and care
> Of Jesus for the men that Pilgrims are!
> Thus to provide! That I should be forgiven!
> And dwell already the next door to heaven!

Then the heavenly sisters will bid you look south from
the top of the House, and you will be thrilled to capacity as
you behold from that peak a more glorious height rising in
the distance before you, the Delectable Mountains, beauti-
fied with woods, vineyards, fruits of all sorts, flowers also,
with springs and fountains.

Thus you will be equipped for the descent into any valley of humiliation. Powers of darkness will surround you,
and Apollyon himself will attack you; but you will have girt
about you the whole armor of God, and you will wax strong in
the power of His might. Those Delectable Mountains you saw in
the distance, which seemed so far out of your grasp, you will
reach joyfully. You will be welcomed there and made to feast
and fellowship royally with Knowledge, Experience, Watchful,
and Sincere. From that peak you will catch a glimpse of the
Celestial City—made of pure gold—and the voice of the loving
Lord, *"Well done."*

Well done, indeed, if you have built upon that foundation—
"gold!"

-4-

Building Silver

Together forever, and not for a day,
We'll gather together forever;
So we will obey, and round Him we'll stay,
And gather His saints all together.
—Author Unknown

You are now upon *the* foundation! And you have been building "gold!" You have been enraptured by the Lord's presence!

"Now if any man build upon this foundation gold, silver. . . ."

If building "gold" is personal, enjoyable, conscious communion with God; what then is building "silver"?

When your heart thrilled under the spell and untranslatable inspiration of the glorious sunrise and your words seemed to stick in your throat with impotency to express your deep feeling, your first reaction was the longing that some kin-soul with sufficient capacity could enter into the indescribable experi-

56

ence with you. Or next best, as the vision lingered in your mind, you exhausted your language powers trying to stir up a sense of your own experience for others. You wanted your closest friends to see what you saw. You wanted them to enjoy the same vision and thrill. And as they entered into some appreciation with you of the vision beautiful, you experienced the maximum of its benefits yourself.

In the "high mountain apart," Peter, James and John saw a vision. It was the Lord "transfigured before them: and His face did shine as the sun, and His raiment was white as the light." Then Peter exclaimed unto Jesus, "Lord, it is good for us to be here: if Thou wilt, let us make here three tabernacles; one for Thee, and one for Moses, and one for Elias" (Matt. 17:4). The double use of that tiny word "us" is very significant. Moved to overflowing by the glory of the transfigured Christ, Peter joyfully shouted, "It is good for *us* to be here." He was happiest in the realization of this high privilege in the fellowship of others— "us." And similarly did Peter desire that joint fellowship in the perpetuating of that miniature heaven here upon the earth— "Let *us* build."

It is our human, or better still, our divine fellow-feeling that urgently craves the fellowship of kindred hearts in sharing our "mountain peak" experiences.

But that is not all. We delight in those that rejoice with us when we rejoice; but we are exceedingly grateful for those that will truly weep with us when we weep. We enjoy those that sing psalms with us when we are merry; we doubly appreciate those that will pray with us when we are afflicted.

I think of the dear heart with whom I had stood upon the transfiguration mount, who was plunged into the thick valley where her heart was sharply anguished as her firstborn infant wavered helplessly in critical condition. That is the time when the ripe fruit of truest fellowship is most essential, and it is also the time when it seems most difficult to help effectually in dulling those sharp arrows of pain.

58

A lone pilgrimage to the Celestial City through earth's uncertain scene is both tragic and severe. Being unable to disclose to some magnanimous heart one's brightest visions, unable to assuage one's bitter grief by pouring out the confused state of mind into some understanding, strong heart is, indeed, distressingly painful.

See Bunyan' pilgrim as he leaves the Palace Beautiful, where he reveled in the ecstatic visions of the glories ahead—he is journeying *alone!* See him as he descends into the valley of humiliation—there to face the cruel enemy, Apollyon, and all his cohorts, *Alone!*

It is not difficult to imagine the great joy that must have been his when the weary pilgrim, Christian, spied ahead of him another of God's honored sons, Faithful. Listen to Christian as he opens the conversation: "My honoured and well beloved Brother *Faithful,* I am glad that I have overtaken you; and that God has so tempered our spirits that we can walk as Companions in this so pleasant a path."

Believers in Christ, whose redeemed spirits have been tempered by God in the school of grace, walking as companions in this so pleasant a path, with its Hill of Difficulty, its valley of Humiliation, its Delectable Mountains, and all the rest, wherein together they may behold the beauty of Him whom they have not seen, and together enjoy and exalt Him whom their hearts truly adore—such blessed Christian fellowship and companionship is building "silver."

WHAT IS CHRISTIAN FELLOWSHIP?

Fellowship signifies "fellows in the same ship." Christian fellowship is a family circle of those who are related through the blood of Jesus Christ, and whose hearts are interwoven with deep family feeling. They unbosom to each other their joys, their sorrows, their cares, and their conflicts. They converse with one another as to the soul's health and progress. And in all their spiritual companionship, the Lord Himself is the center, drawing their hearts together, and the Lord is the circumference, graciously binding them into a communion of saints.

Indeed, we can only have real fellowship one with another as we walk in the immediate presence of God. We cannot build upon the foundation "silver," unless we have built also "gold."

It is interesting to note throughout the Old Testament Scriptures how the use of silver is interconnected with the use of gold, in the making of jewelry, coins, and various treasures. It was used largely also in the fittings of the tabernacle and the temple, but significant is the observation that it occupies a secondary place as compared to the use of gold. And that same ratio must be maintained in the spiritual realities they suggest.

If we build much "gold," we shall thereby be enabled and qualified to build "silver" with our fellow-saints. If the building of "gold" is neglected, then ere long the "silver"—the Christian fellowship—deteriorates into a mere social circle. True Christian fellowship can only be enjoyed in the light of His countenance. "If we walk in the light, as He is in the light, we have fellowship one with another, and the blood of Jesus Christ His Son cleanseth us from all sin" (1 Jn. 1:7). When we are individually walking with God, in the holy privilege of personal communion, we then really have fellowship one with another, and this fellowship consists in a heart enjoyment of Christ as our common portion.

There are many bonds that draw believers one to another; but these, unless they are reinforced by this deepest of all bonds, the affinity of souls, that are moving together in the realm of divine light, are precarious, and apt to snap at the most critical moment. Sin separates men from each other quite as much as it separates each man from God. The one thing that happily brings men together, enabling them to "have fellowship one with another," is not only that each man be embedded in the rock which is the foundation, but also that each one individually walk in the light before God and have fellowship with Him. Common possession of the light and personal fellowship with God—this is the only cement that will perfectly knit Christians to one another.

Sin will naturally and inevitably separate us from God first, turn our hearts toward the darkness, and forthwith break our fellowship one with another. "Two grains of quicksilver laid upon a polished surface will never unite if their surfaces be dusted over with minute impurities, or if the surface of one of them be." Neither will men have the unity of the Spirit among them if they be coated over with a film of sin in the sight of God. But, like the quicksilver, remove the film, and they will freely flow together, coalesce, and be one.

There is a vast amount of mere intercourse among Christians in homes, congregations, and conferences, which has in it not a particle of divine fellowship. "Alas! Alas! A great deal of what passes for Christian fellowship is nothing more than the merest religious gossip—the vapid, worthless, soul-withering chit-chat of the religious world, than which nothing can be more miserably unprofitable. . . . Christian fellowship is not a heartless traffic in certain favorite doctrines which we receive to hold in common. It is not morbid sympathy with those who think and see and feel with us in some favorite theory or dogma. It is something quite different from all this. It is delighting in Christ, in common with all those who are walking in the light. It is attachment to Him, to His person, His Name, His Word, His cause, His people. It is joint consecration of heart and soul to that blessed One who loved us and washed us from our sins in His own blood, and brought us into the light of God's presence, there to walk with Him and with one another"* (*C. H. M. in Miscellaneous Writings*).

In our day, generally speaking, we are inclined to think of fellowship as a mere gossip circle or as some sentimental oneness of people who are listening to Bible preaching. The ordinance of fellowship has been very much neglected. It has

---

* Used by the kind permission of Loizeaux Bros., Inc., New York.

become very difficult for Christian people to speak naturally and spontaneously of the things of Christ to each other. They meet together frequently in the ordinary affairs of life, and they speak avidly of everything except the things most real, that is, those pertaining to their spiritual life; and that, frequently, not because they have not deep experience, not because they are entirely unfamiliar with the things of God, but because somehow they have never been "tempered" to help each other in mutual converse concerning them.

Christians mix and mingle in business affairs and in their churches, but as regarding their inner experiences they pass through life solemn and solitary men, who effectually conceal their hearts as if they were in a descrt, who regard any approach toward fellowship of spirit as an inroad on privacy, and any inquiry for their soul's health as a stranger's intermeddling. They draw themselves into a shell, set upon living their life alone, considering any opening of heart as a weakness. They seem to be quite content without real friends, fellow-helpers, or inner circle of companions—content to pass through life in a smug, spiritual solitude, which even on the surface appears to be rather selfish.

There are Christians, I say, who choose deliberately that type of life, a spiritual aloofness from fellow-believers. On the other hand, there are those like the sincere inquirer after spiritual comfort who said, "It is ten years since I was received a member of a certain church, and during all that time no one has ever said a word to me about my soul." When he was tempted he had to stand alone: if defeated, no one prayed for his restoration. If he triumphed and rejoiced in his victory, he was obliged to hide his peace among his secrets, and could ask no one to rejoice with him. If he had lost his pearl of great price and found it again, he must abide in silence, for his neighbors were not used to being called together to share in another's cares and joys. There is something fearfully chilling in a state of things of which this is too complete a description. It is a woeful fact that in most of our churches we have made a provision for doctrine, for prayers, and for breaking of bread, but none for fellowship. A Christian may be a member of a church and yet be compelled to walk all his way alone, no one knowing or caring to know of his conflicts or his joys.

THE FRUITS OF FELLOWSHIP

Look at the early Christians. Their spiritual life is redolent of family feeling and fellowship. The Word tells us that they continued "steadfast in the apostles' doctrine and fellowship, and in breaking of bread, and in prayers" (Acts 2:42). There are four specific things listed here, and fellowship is one of them. Those early Christians talked together of the interests of their spiritual life, and there really is no surer way to conserve and strengthen the Christian life. Instead of stiff souls always either dressed for the public eye or shut up in silent solitude, you have here brothers, sisters, friends, lovers, clinging to each other in lofty companionship by the mutual attraction of spiritual excellencies. With true family feeling soul meets soul around the fireplace in freedom and frankness between whom the common talk often runs on their salvation, their conflicts, and their glorious foretaste of eternal joy.

Even the Apostles assumed not any of the pseudo-dignity which would prevent touching allusions to personal conviction, to previous experience, and to present spiritual attainments. A babe in Christ was one whose happy experience was a matter for open congratulation by the beloved Apostle, "I write unto you, little children, because your sins are forgiven you, for His name's sake" (1 Jn. 2:12). And the benediction of the Apostle Paul to the church at Corinth breathes also that warm fellowship: "The grace of the Lord Jesus Christ, and the love of God, and the communion of the Holy Ghost, be with you all" (2 Cor. 13:14). Have you ever stopped to think what is meant by "communion of the Holy Ghost"? It is God working in your heart and in my heart, and helping us to enjoy the things of God together in the power of the Holy Spirit. The

Old Testament abounds in gracious illustration of this. Turn to the Psalms, as millions of heaven-bound pilgrims do each day, and at once you are interested, your heart is strangely warmed and drawn heavenward. What is the explanation? It is *not* the spirit of its philosophy, the power of its eloquence, nor yet the charm of its poetry.

It is this. These sublime sonnets disclose the secrets of a man's heart in his communings and complainings before God as he passes through life's joys, sorrows, temptations, wanderings, and deliverances. These soul-autobiographies surge warmly with life's blood. They are real and living, exemplifying here magnificent pathos, there deep depressive feeling, there a searching confession to God, and there ringing with heavenly exuberance. We read them. We sense soul kinship. We experience true companionship. We feel its spiritual breathings entering our forms and enlivening us.

Reconstruct the Psalms on the principle that all about the state of the soul is to be kept in prudent reserve from the knowledge of our brethren, and their life-giving power will vanish.

Turn to the last book of the Old Testament. Cold formalism like an icy pall enveloped the people. The prophet Malachi thundered out the message of God among them. "Then they that feared the Lord spake often one to another." This was not a prayer meeting. It was a fellowship. They spoke to one another and stimulated one another toward diligence and honesty before God.

If we turn from holy writ and look at a reflection in one of its best mirrors, "Pilgrim's Progress," how long would we find delight in it if Bunyan had ordered his pilgrims to close up their bosoms stiffly and prudently? A Christian, a Faithful, a Hopeful, who had nothing to say "one to another" as they traveled on, regarding their escapes, solaces, temptations, and slips—such characters, though they might impress us with airs of some mysterious religionism, would certainly not indulge our sympathetic attention for long.

Indeed, *Mr. Bunyan* has shown us how specific conversation on spiritual issues quickly places the finger on the vital spot. There is Mr. Talkative, who, though fluent on theory and doctrinal points, was very reserved on experiential religion. Faithful, wishing to know how he was to bring him to a point, said to Christian, "What would you have me to do?"

"Why, go to him, and enter into some serious discourse on the power of religion; and ask him plainly, whether this thing be set up in his heart, house, or conversation?"

Faithful, having described how a work of grace "discovers itself when it is in the heart of man," puts to Talkative the plain question, "Do you experience it?"

Talkative at first began to blush, but, recovering himself, replied thus: "You come now to experience, to conscience, and God; and to appeal to Him for justification of what is spoken. This kind of discourse I did not expect; nor am I disposed to give an answer to such questions, because I count not myself bound thereto, unless you take upon you to be a catechizer; and though you should do so, yet I may refuse to make you my judge."

How many professing Christians there are in our day, who, though, perhaps, in many respects different from Mr. Talkative, would fell abashed much as he did if some Faithful came up as close to home on the solid questions of our relation to God.

One reason why spiritual conditions even among Protestants are so deplorable is that these issues are not pondered upon. Formal preaching and teaching, even at best, does not enter as deeply into the soul of man as the edge of personal conversation.

The Christian life will remain comparatively dormant and fruitless, unless it is breathed upon by the bracing influence of human fellowship. Just as the strength and symmetry and beauty of plants are developed by placing them in glass houses, which makes it possible for them on every side to hold fellowship with the spacious sky, even so the seminal powers of our spiritual life and the virtues of our inner capacities become strong and grandly proportioned through a sanctified and sympathetic and spacious communion with our fellow brothers. We are stimulated by the spiritual genius of others. Of all the germs floating around, good and bad, an enthusiastic and solid spirituality is the most contagious. We catch it and unconsciously draw upon the resources of others, and frequently thereby, we are enabled to move forward and even to outsoar our source.

It is not difficult to discover the wells from which *Spenser, Shakespeare, Wordsworth, Tennyson,* and others "fetched" their waters. Their genius found the necessary stimulus in another man's wealth, and they rose to great heights themselves.

Robert Browning, when still but a young man experiencing the surge of poetic awakening, sat up late one night in May, eagerly pouring over the romantic writings of *Shelley* and *Keats*. The imaginative spirituality of Shelley, moving swiftly upon the wings of delicate imagery, startled Browning with delight. For relief from his intellectual and emotional intoxication, he turned to the glowing beauty of Keats' verse expressed in liquid fluency of diction and fluidity of movement. This caused him to soar into worlds equally magnificent. Captivated and enthralled, Browning tarried until the early hours of morning, communing alternately with these two spiritual makers of song and melody. As his spirit burned with eager responsiveness, he heard in a copper-beech at the end of his neighbor's garden two nightingales striving one against the other. Browning's incited fancy imagined for the moment that in the birds were the souls of Keats and Shelley uttering their enfranchised music and welcoming him to drink at the Pierian spring. This was an eventful experience for Browning, who, with "sudden electric tremors," drank the elixir of a new life and descended from transfiguration mount a dedicated spirit commissioned and empowered for the task.

Our hearts are exceedingly sensitive in reacting to the spiritual influences of true spirits. It is said that *Carlyle* and *Tennyson* would spend a whole evening together about the fireplace with but a few pertinent words passed between them. Late at night Carlyle would leave with the remark, "A delightful evening, Tennyson. Good night."—Did he mean it? Of course he did. Two great spirits communed together in deep thought and fellow-feeling.

How wonderful! How stimulating! How spiritually refreshing when our voices blend, our praise, our petitions harmonize, and our spirits in worship together are subdued and nourished by the glorious presence of God.

"O magnify the Lord with me, and let us exalt His name together" (Psa. 34:3). This is the cry of souls possessed by the spirit of praise, yearning to have fellowship with others of like mind. The Apostle Paul suggests some further instructions as to how we may have the "fellowship of the Spirit" in magnifying unitedly the Lord: "If there be therefore any consolation in Christ, if any comfort of love, if any fellowship of the Spirit, if any bowels and mercies, fulfill ye my joy, that ye be like-minded, having the same love, being of one accord, of one mind. Let nothing be done through strife or vainglory; but in lowliness of mind let each esteem other better than themselves. Look not every man on his own things, but every man also on the things of others" (Phil. 2:1-4). This is a warning against the "perils of self-centeredness." It is an appeal for us to get the other person's point of view, to survey his outlook, and to realize the condition of his life—"every man also [to look] on the things of others."

Life is exceedingly complex, and even within the limits of one congregation, you will find varied needs and experiences: some are struggling in the Slough of Despond, others undergoing the "trembling rejoicing" right after passing through the Wicket-Gate. Some are climbing the Hill Difficulty with its crouching lions; others are resting sweetly in the chamber called "Peace" within the Palace Beautiful. Some are descending the irksome Valley of Humiliation, and others are already in fierce combat with Apollyon. Some are enduring the glittering temptations of Vanity

Fair; others are already singing in the bright land of Beulah. Some are just beginning the pilgrimage, with all the perils ahead; and others are on the brink of the river, with all the dangers behind them. How widely separated and different the needs of Christian pilgrims can be. It is quite obvious that our spiritual sympathy must have ample spontaneity and elasticity, if we are effectually "to look also on the things of others," and contribute helpfully toward a real spiritual fellowship.

In the preceding chapter one thread was dropped, which can be picked up here. We noticed in Psalm 34:12 a summation of the "abundant life." In verse 9 we noticed how reverencing and enjoying the Lord is the taproot of that life. In verses 13 and 14 we see the fruitage of the "life abundant," that is, fellowshipping profitably with other believers.

The exhortation of verses 13 and 14 is largely of a negative character, but it does lead up to the positive and the nourishing aspects of Christian brotherhood: "Keep thy tongue from evil, and thy lips from speaking guile. Depart from evil, and do good; seek peace, and pursue it."

Christian, be careful to heed this vital counsel of keeping your lips and tongue from evil and injurious uses. The fellowship of believers is a garden full of delicate plants, whose leafage and blossoms must not be exposed to the withering blasts of evil speaking and slanderous insinuations. Flee from those possessed of these blighting habits, engage yourself actively, Christian, in doing good and speaking lovely words of encouragement, if you are to drink the refreshing cordials of brotherly communing.

There is one way in which we can keep ourselves from the destructiveness of those withering words sounded in caustic criticisms, suspicions raised about this one and that one, and slandering remarks indulged in about others. I suggest, there is one way in which we can keep from that and use our precious moments together more profitably for all concerned—and that is by using our time and energies as the Psalmist suggested, "to magnify the Lord," and to "exalt His name together." But how can this be done. Well, notice further in that same Psalm the kind of fellowship that was enjoyed in a united testimony and adoration. They joined in an outburst of jubilant rejoicing, each one contributing his own testimony, and each one spiritually revived by the expressions of the others.

"I sought the Lord and He heard me, and delivered me from all my fears" (Psa. 34:4), says one person. He is praising the Lord for delivering him from the jaws of fear.

Another little company testifies as follows: "They looked unto Him, and were lightened: and their faces were not ashamed" (Psa. 34:5). They were losing heart, but the Lord brought into their midst a benediction of light.

And the thankful confession of the third runs like this: "This poor man cried, and the Lord heard him, and saved him out of all his troubles" (Psa. 34:6). He had been in a tight place, and the Lord graciously intervened in his behalf.

Then together they harmonize an expression of praise to the Lord, "The angel of the Lord encampeth round about them that fear Him, and delivereth them" (Psa 34:7).

Here is an example of true and profitable Christian fellowship about the person of Christ. Such sympathetic and sincere fellowship is a great spiritual ministry which helps our brothers who may be experiencing other needs, and at the same time it enriches ourselves. "The violin gains something from an accompaniment," observes *J. H. Jowett;* "each instrument in the orchestra is enriched by the co-operation of the others. Each member in a chorus has his discernment sharpened, and his zeal intensified by the remaining members. So it is in the orchestra of praise. My own thanksgiving is quickened and enriched when I join it to the praises of others. My own note is gladdened. My eagerness is inflamed."

Harmonizing together in spiritual things for the glory of God, "teaching and admonishing one another in psalms and hymns and spiritual songs, singing with grace in your hearts to the Lord"

(Col. 3:16)—this is building "silver."

Christians, banded together in small groups or in congregations, are to constitute a fellowship for the spiritual encouragement of all; they are to "speak often one to another ... exhort one another ... confess their faults one to another, and pray for one another." This is the kind of thing that many believers daily hunger for and seek after.

How many of us have not driven fifty or a hundred miles or more some evening to be a short time with some spiritually understanding friend, so that we could unburden to him the heavy load due to failure, or pour out the heart in sincere rejoicing, and then together draw nigh unto the throne of grace in petition and praise. This becomes a spiritual oasis. One could approach the Lord alone, but we crave and are wonderfully stimulated by that precious companionship of kindred hearts. Precious boon! Thrice blessed privilege! Unhappy, indeed, is he who in his circle of friends does not have at least one tried and true spiritual companion.

This is the God-designed means of grace not only for the individual strengthening of the believers, but also for the edification of the whole body of Christ. In speaking concerning the edifying of the body of Christ, the Apostle Paul said, "But speaking the truth in love," (we) "may grow up into Him in all things, which is the head, even Christ: from whom the whole body fitly joined together and compacted by that which every joint supplieth, according to the effectual working in the measure of every part, maketh increase of the body unto the edifying of itself in love" (Eph. 4:15, 16). Here we see how "every joint" and "every part" is to make certain contributions and thus to perform an effectual working for a building up of the whole body of Christ.

"Fitly joined together and compacted by that which every joint supplieth." This brings to my attention *Hebich's* Tub. Shall I bring it out? Well, here it is: *Samuel Hebich*, a German missionary on the west coast of India, stirred many hearts with searching questions and tender expositions of the Word. He delighted to read the fourth chapter of Ephesians and expound it carefully till he came to the sixteenth verse, which he read slowly, and repeated the words, *"fitly shoined togeder."*

(I will give it to you as nearly as possible in his own language. His English has force.)

He paused a few seconds, and abruptly put the question, "Did you ever see a tob?" This homely appeal roused the audience, and caused some smiling.

"If you go to a tob factory, you vill see some fery large tobs. You and I cannot make a tob: it requires a cood carpenter to make a tob, or it vill hold no vater, because it is not made of von peece of ood, but of many, and de many must be *fitly shoined togeder.* There are four tings to make a cood tob.

"1. It must have a coot bottom.
"2. Each of de peeces must be fitly shoined to de bottom.
"3. Each von must be fitly shoined to his fellow.
"4. Each von shall be kept close by de bands outside.

"Von peece may be narrow and the next peece be vide, yet it shall be a cood tob, but if a leetle shtone or bit of shtick vill come between de peeces, it vill not do at all. Now, if vee haf a cood bottom, and efry peece be fitly shoined to de bottom, and all are fitly shoined togeder from de top to de bottom, haf vee not a tob? No, it vill not hold vater for von moment till de bands are put on. De bands press hard each peece of ood and den are dey more fitly shoined togeder.

" 'Oder foundation can no man lay den dat is laid, vich is Jesus Christ.' Here vee haf de cood bottom for our tob, it is perfect; and efry von dat truly believes is resting on dis cood bottom, and is fitly shoined to it by de Holy Spirit of God. Dere are many who call demselves Christians who are not shoined, but vee are not speaking of dem now.

"In de Acts of de Apostles vee read often of being 'filled vit de Holy Ghost,' and ven gadered togeder for prayer vonce, de whole house did shake vid His power. But dis is not alvays. Vy not? Vee shall see. Vat is de shmall shtick or shtone between de peeces of ood dat make de tob? It is de *leetle quarrel,*—de *hard vord,*—de *dirty bit of money,* dat keeps broder from being fitly shoined to broder. Vat is de space between de peeces from top to bottom, troo vich you can see de light? It is de *coldness* dat you feel but do not tell. Vat is de peece of ood that falls out de circle? It is the *proud, unforgiving spirit* dat efry von can feel is in de meeting, and vich causes all heavenly peece to run out."

Now listen to Hebich's earnest conclusion, so very needful in every fellowship:

"Oh, beloved, be *fitly shoined togeder!* You haf no power of your own. Dat vich shall keep you is de *encircling bands* of de love of Jesus, from head to foot, and as dis power presses on each of you, so vill you become yet more closely shoined togeder. Den de Holy Spirit shall fill you to overflowing. Den all who come into your midst shall be refreshed, and de name of de Lord Jesus be glorified!"*

The body of Christ is in truth edified by that which "every joint" supplieth—contributes—if the members are "fitly joined together." When the Holy Spirit takes away from our hearts the starch, selfishness, yea, the sin, our stiffness will give way to warm companionship and discerning sympathy with others of the fold.

Since we are "knit TOGETHER" (Col. 2:2), "fitly framed and joined TOGETHER" (Eph. 2:21), "tempered TOGETHER" (1 Cor. 12:24), being "followers TOGETHER" (Phil. 3:17), let us in unity dwell TOGETHER (Psa. 133:1), strive TOGETHER (Phil. 1:27), commune TOGETHER (Luke 24:15), labor and work TOGETHER (2 Cor. 6:1), and rejoice TOGETHER (Rom. 12:15).

Since God has "quickened us TOGETHER," "raised us

* From the tract, "Hebich's Tub." Used by the kind permission of Loizeaux Brothers, Inc., New York.

TOGETHER," "made us sit TOGETHER" (Eph. 2:5, 6), and exalted us to be "heirs TOGETHER" (1 Pet. 3:7), let us, therefore, be "comforted TOGETHER" (Rom. 1:12), waiting to be "caught up TOGETHER" (1 Thess. 4:17), "glorified TOGETHER" (Rom. 8:17), and for all eternity to "live TOGETHER" (1 Thess. 5:10).

And TOGETHER until then, "building silver."

This precious, much-needed value we may mint together about the Throne of Grace as we journey on.

Say often one to another, "Do you know the Lord?" Is He precious to you?" and "Are you enjoying His blessed fellowship?" Gaze together upon His countenance, and be at peace one with another.

You will reap and relish the ripe fruit of brotherly companionship. You will intensify one another's spiritual capacities as you behold the beauty of the Lord together. Your faith, too, will be strengthened so that you will be enabled to help and comfort the distracted mother in the valley below.

Thus, even thus, building upon the foundation "silver!"

-5-

Building Precious Stones

Only like souls I see the folk thereunder,
  Bound who should conquer, slaves who should be kings,—
Hearing their one hope with an empty wonder,
  Sadly contented in a show of things;—

Then with a rush the intolerable craving
  Shivers throughout me like a trumpet-call,—
Oh, to save these! To perish for their saving,
  Die for their life, be offered for them all!

—F. W. H. Myers

"Now if any man build upon that foundation gold, silver, precious stones . . . ."

Be still with thy God alone. Thrill at His presence with you. Permit Him to enjoy the trophy of His grace. This is the *greatest* thing you can do for God. It is building upon the foundation "gold!"

Believers in Christ together about the table in some Palace Beautiful rehearsing the goodness of the Lord, or upon the slopes of some Hill Difficulty comforting one another and praying one for another, or together upon the pinnacle of the Hill

Clear peering into the glories of the Celestial City and rejoicing calmly in that blessed hope! This is the greatest thing Christians can do one for another. With such fellowship God is well pleased. There the Holy Spirit presides with power and dignity and blessing. This is building "silver."

And would you render worthwhile and permanent service to the world—to those outside of the Shepherd's fold and the Church's fellowship? The greatest thing you can do there is to point them personally to the Lord Jesus Christ as Savior. This is their supreme need. This is your greatest service. This is building "precious stones!"

The members of the body of Christ, the Church, are called "living stones," as contributing to the building of that living temple of which Christ Himself is the chief Corner Stone (Eph. 2:20-22; 1 Pet 2:4-8). Precious stones are frequently alluded to in Scripture and were used on the high priest's breastplate for engraving upon each one the name of one of the tribes. "Precious stones are used in Scripture in a figurative sense," says Peloubet's Dictionary, "to signify value, beauty, durability, etc., in those objects with which they are compared."

Value! Is there anything on the face of the earth excelling in value the worth of a human soul? We gasp at the works of men in spanning land and sea with highways, rail, bridges, planes, and ships. We exclaim at the luxuriousness of his house and other belongings. What is the value we actually place upon his soul? *Daniel Webster* (1782-1852), one day, walking along the streets of a small New England town, met a little boy, and, we are told, took off his hat to the boy. When asked why he did so, he replied, "I did so when I thought of the wonderful possibilities wrapped up in that little brain and upon what it would unfold in its generation."

How much more awe-stricken you and I might stand in the presence of an immortal soul! Think about it just a moment—an eternal soul. That soul came from God, and to God it must return for accounting. For that soul Christ made plenteous redemption in His substitutionary death and His triumphant resurrection. That soul is today being constantly pursued by the Holy Spirit, who by every means is striving to arouse it to a sense of its need of Christ, to reveal Christ to it, the one Mediator, and to energize it to accept Him as Savior and Lord. In the presence of the angels of God there is great rejoicing when one soul is born anew and fitted for heaven. All the forces of evil, on earth and in the heavenlies, are arrayed with fearful cruelty and hellish deceptions to keep that soul from God and in every way to stunt and dwarf its spiritual progress.

And no one can better evaluate the preciousness of the human soul than that soul's greatest Lover. No one can as fully fathom the gravity of that soul's unending destiny as can the Eternal Christ. And we do not wonder nor consider an exaggeration His evaluation of that soul when He said, "What shall it profit a man, if he gain the whole world, and lose his own soul? Or what shall a man give in exchange for his soul?" (Mk. 8:36, 37).

The *beauty* and *durability* of the "precious stones" also fittingly describe the soul. It is created in the image of God. Sin's hideousness has not been permitted to blot out entirely the likeness of the original. Its beauty is incomparable. Its powers of reason, its warmth of affection, its sense of discrimination, its faculty of volition, and its capability of appreciation—these qualities alone make the delicacy and beauty of the human soul to excel everything else on the face of the earth as much as the heavens are high above the earth. And it shall never pass away into nothingness. It has a beginning, but it knows no ending.

An immortal soul! Who can compute its value, or describe its beauty, or measure its durability? An immortal soul now dwells in every boy and girl, man and woman in whose nostrils still is the breath of life. Omit to reckon the value of the soul, and the human person is worth less than a dollar when the chemicals that go into the composition of the average body are salvaged.

"He which converteth the sinner from the error of his way shall save a soul from death" (Jas. 5:20). Shall save a *soul* from death. Would to God that we could realize the meaning of it. Death is one of the most awful words in the English language. And note please, that it speaks of the death of the "soul," not of the body. It means for that soul everlasting separation from God and exposed forever to the wrath of God. When the veil of bodily death has rent the curtain which hides eternal things, we shall enter into the realm of sight, the believer to see his Lord eternally, and the unsaved to discover that the warnings of God in His Word were all solemnly true.

There is not one Scripture in the whole Bible upon which we can build the slightest hope of the future salvation of an unbeliever who passes out of this world without Christ. "He that believeth not the Son shall not see life, but the wrath of God abideth on him" (Jn. 3:36). That eternal issue of the soul is a matter of individual choice here and now. Eternal life for those who receive the Lord Jesus Christ, or eternal ruin for those who reject Him.

Oh, to be used of God in saving souls from death. They are all about us every day. Think also to *what* that soul is saved: Saved to holiness; saved to glory; saved to likeness of Christ.

To snatch an immortal soul from sin and the never-ending blackout of hell by pointing it to the all-sufficient and all-abiding Savior is, by any standard of measurement and under any circumstances, the most honorable and the most holy service that can be rendered to those in the world. There is nothing surpassing it by any stretch of the imagination. A soul quickened with life divine and translated from the "kingdom of darkness" into the "kingdom of light" is the most brilliant conception. It is eternally profitable to men. It is pleasing to God. It is sweet and precious. The wisest man spoke wisest wisdom when the Holy Spirit bade him say that "The fruit of the righteous is a tree of life;

and he that winneth souls is wise" (Prov. 11:30). To win souls seems to be the ripest and the chiefest fruit which the trees of righteousness, that is the believers, can bear in time. It is the wisest end to which wisdom can be put. Winning souls is the acme of wisdom. Such wisdom is "more precious than rubies."

Wouldn't it be remarkable if you could go out into the mud, pick out an ordinary stone, and, by some strange art of the lapidary, transform that stone into a diamond? But that is nothing compared with going down into the mud of sin, picking out of it lost men and women and boys and girls, and, by the divine art of the soul winner, transforming them, through the grace of God, into jewels worthy of a place in the Savior's diadem.

In monuments of marble we commemorate the deeds of the great for a few years; but a soul won through your instrumentality will in itself be a monument of that fact forever. You may build for yourself an everlasting memorial in Zion. It is thus that "the righteous shall be in everlasting remembrance" (Psa. 112:6).

Be wise! Build for eternity "precious stones" upon that foundation which God has laid. Consider the instruction and the encouragement of Daniel, who said, "They that be wise shall shine as the brightness of the firmament; and they that turn many to righteousness as the stars for ever and ever" (12:3). It is quite natural with all of us to want to "shine," to want to build, to accomplish something worth while.

Some there are who are interested only in shining here in this world, and for that purpose exhaust all their talents and energies. And, lo, the succeeding generation sighs over that awful waste. It does not pay to shine here. "The brightest star in any galaxy of earthly glory soon fades." The brightest stars in the glamorous circles of society, the brightest stars in the fascinating financial world, the brightest stars in the intriguing world of sports—they all are quickly forgotten; their wonderful faces are only grinning skulls; their fair forms are ungainly skeletons. "For all flesh is as grass, and all the glory of man as the flower of grass. The grass withereth, and the flower thereof falleth away" (1 Pet. 1:24). It does not pay to burn yourself up shining down here. It leaves but dust and ashes and an empty name "writ in water" on the tombstone.

But they that turn many to righteousness are as the brightness of the firmament, and shall shine as the stars forever and ever. There is only one way to shine up yonder—only *one* way—and that is by winning souls to Christ.

Wearied and worn with earthly cares, I yielded to repose,
    And soon before my raptured sight a glorious vision rose.
I thought, whilst slumbering on my couch, in midnight's solemn gloom
    I heard an angel's silv'ry voice, and radiance filled my room
A gentle touch awakened me,—a gentle whisper said,
    "Arise, O sleeper, follow me," and through the air we fled.

We left the earth so far away, that like a speck it seemed,
    And heavenly glory, calm and pure, across our pathway streamed.
Still on we went,—my soul was wrapt in silent ecstacy;
    I wondered what the end would be, what next should meet mine eye.
I knew now how we journeyed through the pathless fields of light,
    When suddenly a change was wrought, and I *was clothed in white.*

We stood before a city's walls most glorious to behold;
    We passed through gates of glistening pearl, o'er streets of purest gold;
It needed not the sun by day, the silver moon by night;
    The glory of the Lord was there, the Lamb Himself its light.
Bright angels paced the shining streets, sweet music filled the air,
    And white-robed saints with glitt'ring crowns, from ev'ry clime were there;

And some that I had loved on earth stood with them round the throne,
    "All worthy is the Lamb," they sang, "the glory His alone."
But fairer far than all beside, I saw my Savior's face;
    And as I gazed He smiled on me with wondrous love and grace.

Lowly I bowed before His throne, o'erjoyed that I at last
    Had gained the object of my hopes; that earth at length was past,
And then in solemn tones He said, "Where is the diadem
    That ought to sparkle on thy brow—adorned with many a gem?
I know thou hast believed on Me, and life through Me is thine,
    But where are all those radiant stars that in thy crown should shine?
Yonder thou seest a glorious throng, and stars on every brow;
    For ev'ry soul they led to Me they wear a jewel now!

And such *thy* bright reward had been if such had been thy *deed*,
    If thou hadst sought some wand'ring feet in path of peace to lead
I did not mean that thou should'st tread the way of life *alone*,
    But that the clear and shining light which round thy footsteps shone
Should guide some other weary feet to My bright home of rest,
    And thus in blessing those around, thou hadst thyself been blest."

The vision faded from my sight, the voice no longer spake,
    A spell seemed brooding o'er my soul which long I feared to break
And when at last I gazed around, in morning's glimm'ring light,
    My spirit fell o'erwhelmed beneath that vision's solemn sight.
I rose and wept with chastened joy that yet I dwelt below,
    That yet another hour was mine my faith by works to show;
That yet some sinner I might tell of Jesus' dying love,
    And help to lead some weary soul to seek a home above.

And now, while on the earth I stay, my motto this shall be,—
    "To live no longer to myself, but Him Who died for me!"
And graven on my inmost soul this word of truth divine,—
    They that turn many to the Lord bright as the stars shall shine.

                    —Author Unknown

"He that is wise winneth souls." Such wisdom is "more precious than rubies." And he that is wise and winneth souls is building upon that foundation . . . precious stones. This is, indeed, a "pearl of great price."

Most Christians are busy with some form of so-called Christian service. They are running hither and thither, attending committee meetings, giving socials, teaching, speaking, preaching. They are covered up with much excellent activity week after week. They are advancing themselves and gaining recognition. The work is gaining in stature. But, alas, they are not winning souls to the Lord Jesus Christ. "The *supreme business* of believers is winning souls to Jesus Christ. A godly life, one that is free from willful sin, is one that abounds in joy and constantly experiences the fulfillment of God's promises in matters of personal victories and the supply of all needs, *but* God's *purposes* are not being fulfilled in any believer who is not actually winning souls to Jesus Christ." I found this crisp statement in the personal papers of *Rev. T. J. Tanner*, in writing *A Pattern of Good Works*, the biography of this choice spirit, who now shines among the brightest of all those who have been called yonder from God's regiment on earth known as Cumberland Presbyterians.

Do not our hearts become restless within us when we realize that in our Christian service we are missing the purpose of God by failing to lead souls to the Lord Jesus Christ? And this becomes our urgent question: "How may I win souls?"

The Bible abounds with instructions and illustrations on the subject of soul-winning. In Psalm 126, we find not only God's way of winning souls clearly laid out, but also the history of a redeemed soul.

See first of all how accurately and beautifully that which was written concerning the returned exiles of Judah describes the history and reactions of the redeemed soul:

When the Lord turned again the captivity of Zion,
we were like them that dream.
Then was our mouth filled with laughter, and
our tongue with singing: then said they among the
heathen, the Lord hath done great things for them.
The Lord hath done great things for us; whereof
we are glad.
Turn again our captivity, O Lord, as the
streams in the south.
They that sow with tears shall reap in joy. (Psa. 126:1-5).

"When the Lord turned again the captivity of Zion." The release of Judah from the Babylonian captivity here referred to illustrates the deliverance of the soul from the bondage of sin and law and death into the glorious liberty of the sons of God. It was *the Lord* who turned the captivity. The soul passed from death unto life. It was the Lord's doing. It is marvelous in our eyes.

It seemed almost too good to be true: "We are like them that dream." The soul became enraptured in the realization of what God had done for it. The reactions and results are quite notable. There was exuberant joy on the part of the believer: "Then was our mouth filled with laughter, and our tongue with singing." Even the heathen, the unsaved round about them, were impressed by the God-wrought emancipation: "Then said they among the heathen, The Lord hath done great things for them." And when the happy freedmen heard this, they exclaimed with one consent, "The Lord hath done great things for us; whereof we are glad."

Joyfully and triumphantly, the people of Judah returned to their own beloved land. But the sight of ruined cities and villages and vineyards caused tears to flow freely, and the mourning well-nigh choked the newfound joy of being freed from the yoke of Babylon. But they did not abandon themselves to aggravated grief. They cried earnestly to the Lord, "Turn again our captivity, O Lord, as the streams in the south." They commenced their diligent labors even as they prayed. And, though with tears, they plowed, they harrowed, they sowed. God did cause the nourishing streams from the south to flow. And they who sowed in tears came forth reaping with joy.

All over our land today we see a spiritual desolation more grievous than what Judah beheld in its ancient land. Our hearts are cold, our churches are formal, our prayers are powerless, our preaching is vapid. The Bible, even where it is still reverenced as the Word of God, seems to be a dull Book. Our singing has gradually changed themes and has become spiritless. We feel the scorching drought of worldliness all about us. Our souls yearn for the refreshing dews from heaven. The Holy Spirit must brood over us, revive our spirits, and turn again our captivity. We must again be moved to go out sowing with tears, ere we can reap with joy. Soul-winning must become our chief concern.

"He that goeth forth and weepeth, bearing precious seed, shall doubtless come again with rejoicing, bringing his sheaves with him" (Psa. 126:6). This verse gives the five DIVINE IN-GREDIENTS in Soul-Winning:

(1) "He that goeth forth"—the COMPELLING
    IMPERATIVE—G O

(2) "And weepeth"—THE COMPASSIONATE HEART
(3) "Bearing precious seed"—THE LIFE-LATENT
SEED—The Word of God
(4) "Shall doubtless come again . . . bringing sheaves"—
THE ABIDING ASSURANCE OF RESULTS
(5) "With rejoicing bringing his sheaves with him"—
THE INCENTIVE OF HOME-COMING

The Compelling Imperative—G O

The first requisite in soul-winning is G O— "He that goeth forth." This is the marching order of the Captain of our Salvation; "Go ye therefore" (Matt. 28:19), "Go ye into all the world" (Mk. 16:15). We must actually get at it, not simply think about it, talk about it, and plan it all out for some more propitious tomorrow. We all know Christians who pray, read the Bible, exercise diligence in their daily walk, attend church, yet never win a soul. These good folk generally excuse themselves on the ground that if they live a good life and set a good example, it should be enough, and that by that means sinners should be led to Christ. The influence of a godly life in this regard must not be minimized, but the facts reveal that much more is necessary than the example. We must go to them and approach them directly on the subject of their salvation. That's the way you and I were saved. Someone came and spoke to us.

Dr. Wilton Merle Smith tells how, while at Princeton Seminary one day, he resolved to speak to at least one person about the claims of Christ before retiring that night. He said it was the most miserable day he ever spent. He put in the whole forenoon without speaking to his men. In the afternoon he became more miserable still. At supper he had one good opportunity and did not use it. He went out into the night, walking back and forth on the campus, fighting, fighting, fighting. He kept saying to himself, "I am a man of my word, but how shall I do it?'

He saw a light up in the third story in the window of the room of a man over whom he had some influence on the baseball team.

He fought his way up one flight, and then up the second, and there he had the hardest fight. He got up to the third floor, stood in front of the door and had another terrible struggle. Then he hit the door, and it flew open. His friend noticed right off that some strange mission brought him and said, "What's the matter, Wilton? What's the matter with you?" He said, "I have come to ask you why you don't become a Christian." His fellow-student broke into tears, strong man that he was, and said, "I have been waiting here for hours for you to come and ask me that question."

Henry Clay Trumbull (1872-1941) made this accurate observation, "Believe me, those who do not know Christ do not resent our talking to them about the Lord, provided we mean what we say. They do resent cant and hypocrisy and sham, but they do not resent our talking to them about things that hold us and move us. They wonder that we do not speak about these things." There is no substitute for the "go" in soul-winning. There is no possible excuse for not doing it. We must always be going forth. We must "be instant in season" and "out of season" (2 Tim. 4:2). Effective soul winners are those who go when it is convenient and go also when it is not convenient. And it is to the "Goer" in soul-winning that Christ pledged His abiding presence, "and, lo, I am with you alway, even unto the end of the world" (Matt. 28:19, 20).

When the Lord commissioned the deacon Philip to go unto the Gaza desert on soul-winning business, saying, "Arise and go . . . ," Philip obeyed promptly: "And he arose and went."

Let us arise from whatever we may be doing and go after those who are lost. It should always be our paramount business. A gentleman offered a gospel tract to a lady in a train, and received the withering reply, "Please attend to your own business." "That's exactly what I'm doing, madam," he replied: "my business is to save souls from death." May this primary ingredient in soul-winning, indeed, be to us a compelling imperative, shivering within us like a trumpet call, impelling us to GO and "by all means save some" (1 Cor. 9:22).

THE COMPASSIONATE HEART

"And weepeth." "He that goeth forth and weepeth." Weeping suggests deep earnestness, a genuine concern and a holy enthusiasm, all of which are essential in the one who would urge the mercy of God and the claims of Christ upon the lost. All other approaches, all other means prove inadequate if this heart-felt concern for their souls be lacking. Its presence is readily detected, and the absence of it just as quickly noted. All schemes, all plans, all efforts in soulwinning become but profitless humdrum, unless the love of God is shed abroad in the heart of the personal worker, constraining him to seek and to win souls for Christ.

A man in a penitentiary once wrote *Dr. Clarence Macartney* a letter as follows:

"First. Can anything be done for a man like *me*? I have sinned 'against light,' and in the face of scores of opportunities to be straight. 'All hope gone' is the phrase that most accurately sets forth *my* feelings.

"Second. I *do not* believe that professedly Christian people feel any deep concern for my soul. Many men and women who never go near a church are moved with the ordinary feelings of charity and humanity—even pagans feel that!—But I *do not* believe that anybody has any real 'burden' for my soul. If I did—well, the evidence of *just one* such case would be enough to make me completely change my life at any cost!

"Do you personally know any 'Christian' man or woman who has the real thing? If so, I wish you would have that man or woman write me."*

This man, like the Psalmist, not only knew his aching void, but also peculiarly sensed the chilling circumstance that "no man cared for my soul" (Psa. 142:4). He was probably right in his bitter presumption. Oh, how few there are who do care for souls. We must have the compassionate heart, the broken heart,

* From MACARTNEY'S ILLUSTRATIONS, by Clarence Edward Macartney. Copyright 1945 by Whitmore and Stone. Used by permission of the publisher, Abingdon—Cokesbury Press.

the weeping heart; and it is this Spirit-energized tenderness that stirs irresistibly the wandering, and, like a magnet, will strangely pull at the heart of the coldest and hardest of unbelievers.

Fanny Crosby, the blind song writer, was at the McAuley Mission. She asked if there was a boy there who had no mother, and if he would come up and let her lay her hand on his head. The motherless little fellow came up, and she put her arms about him and kissed him.

They parted; she went from the meeting and wrote that inspiring song, "Rescue the Perishing"; and when *Mr. Sankey* was about to sing the song in St. Louis, he related the incident. A man sprang to his feet in the audience and said, "I am the boy she kissed that night. I never was able to get away from the impression made by that touching act, until I became a Christian. I am now living in this city with my family, am a Christian, and am doing a good business."

> Lead me to some soul today,
> O teach me Lord just what to say;
> Friends of mine are lost in sin,
> And cannot find their way.
> Few there are who seem to care,
> And few there are who pray;
> Melt my heart and fill my life,
> Give me one soul today.
>
> —*Will H. Houghton**

The example of Christ is above all others. He who came to "seek and to save that which was lost" (Lu. 19:10) made that His urgent business all His days on earth. Under all sorts of circumstances He carried on His work with individuals. While ministering to large crowds, He would focus His attention upon some individual. Always His heart was yearning for their souls. To the lips of the much-married Samaritan woman He pressed the water of life. The two searching followers of John the Baptist followed Him to His lodging and became convinced. The moneymaking publican, Matthew, was stirred by those two never-to-be-forgotten words of the Lord, "Follow me." Upon

* Used by the kind permission of Moody Press, Chicago.

Nicodemus, the religious leader, Christ urged, "You must be born again."

He spied the little man Zacchaeus, up in the tree, went to his house, and witnessed a completely transformed life. He answered the simple faith of the lepers, the blind, the halt, the maimed, yea, even the one who touched the hem of His garment, and made them whole in spirit as well as in body. And His last recorded act, as He was stretched out upon the cross, was personal work with the dying thief. His compassionate heart was moved exceedingly for the gainsayers, the hardened, the bigoted, the unbelievers; and He wept bitterly, "O Jerusalem, Jerusalem, thou that killest the prophets, and stonest them which are sent unto thee, how often would I have gathered thy children together, even as a hen gathereth her chickens under her wings, and ye would not!" (Matt. 23:37).

And then we see in the New Testament how the Apostles and others imitated the example of Christ. Andrew led Peter to Christ; Philip led Nathanael to Him. Peter and John alone dealt with the lame man at the gate called Beautiful; and Philip, the deacon, left a flourishing revival work in a large city, followed the Spirit's leading to the desert of Gaza, and "ran" to join himself to the chariot of an Ethiopian prince riding along, reading from the prophet Isaiah. He pointed him to Christ as Savior and enabled him to go into the dark continent as a flaming light for Christ.

We note that Ananias had the rare honor of ushering Paul into the full light of the gospel. We see how Aquila and Priscilla showed unto the eloquent Apollos the way of the Lord more perfectly.

Look for a moment at Paul and the other missionaries, who covered every corner of the inhabited earth with the gospel. To the Ephesian elders Paul could say, "Remember, that by the space of three years I ceased not to warn every one night and day with tears" (Acts 20:31). With a broken, shepherd's heart, he went "from house to house" showing and teaching to them Christ (Acts 20:20). So burdened was Paul for the souls of his kinsmen that he was, indeed, willing "to perish for their saving, die for their life." "I say the truth in Christ," he said; "I lie not, my conscience also bearing me witness in the Holy Ghost, that I have great heaviness and continual sorrow in my heart. For I could wish that myself were accursed from Christ for my brethren, my kinsmen according to the flesh" (Rom. 9:1-3). The constant persecutions, the stoning, the imprisonments, the lashes, the accusations, the trying voyages, shipwrecks and all—none of these things cooled his devotion to Christ, nor his zeal for the lost.

Soul-winning was not limited to the Apostles. In Acts 8 we read that "they that were scattered abroad went everywhere preaching the gospel." This included all except the Apostles. All believers engaged zealously in personal work. *Gibbon* attributes the wide and rapid diffusion of the gospel of Christ in those early days to the fact that "it became the most sacred duty of a new convert to diffuse among his friends the inestimable blessing which he had received."

Great soul-winners in all ages had a similar burning passion. Moody felt that he was an utter failure unless he could speak each day to at least one person about his soul. *John Smith*, the mighty Wesleyan preacher, used to say, "I am a brokenhearted man; not for myself, but on account of others. God has given me such a sight of the value of precious souls that I cannot live if souls are not saved. Oh, give me souls, or else I die!"

Believers in Christ! To the work! To the work! Let us again speak every man to his neighbor, "Know you the Lord." And may it be done with Christ-like tenderness and compassion and tears. The tears of the weeping prophet Jeremiah melted many of his sin-hardened kinsmen, "Oh that my head were waters, and mine eyes a fountain of tears, that I might weep day and night for the slain of the daughter of my people!" (9:1). The tears of Hezekiah touched and moved the heart of God: "Go, and say to Hezekiah, Thus saith the Lord, the God of David thy father, I have heard thy prayer, I have seen thy tears: behold, I will add unto thy days fifteen years" (Isa. 38:5).

The pearl is produced by suffering. When a small grain of sand comes between the shell and the body of the oyster, the oyster suffers severe pain, and this causes the body to give off a fluid which crystallizes around the grain to remove the pain, and this becomes the pearl. Even so, suffering and tears and a broken heart are essential ingredients in the production of "precious stones."

THE LIFE-LATENT SEED—THE WORD OF GOD

"He that goeth forth and weepeth, bearing precious seed." He who would reap a harvest of souls for glory must first of all plant the precious seed, which is the Word of God. God's Word, as recorded in the Bible, alone has the divine power latent in it to produce the desired results of regeneration and all the spiritual blessings that follow. In interpreting the parable of the Sower and the Seed, Christ told us that "The seed is the Word of God" (Lu. 8:11).

In that same parable Christ analyzed the wide range of circumstances and temperaments of the masses of hearers into four kinds of soil. Those into whom we would inject the "precious seed" are one of the following:

> Wayside—Indifferent, hardened;
> Stony—Superficial, shallow;
> Thorny—Preoccupied, distracted;
> Good—Productive, devout.

Indeed, a variety of conditions, but still the Word of God is the best seed for all the temperaments. In all the many different situations that we come upon, there can never be any substitute for the Word of God. The resources of our abilities, the schemings of our tact, the magnetism of our personality must never be permitted to crowd out the Word of God. Human wisdom and learning and philosophizing cannot take the place of the revelation of God in His Word. That is why

Dr. Walter A. Maier (1893-1950), of the Lutheran Hour, strives to give out at least one verse of Scripture for every minute that his message is on the air.

And even relating our own experiences in the things of God must be carefully watched, and used only where it will illustrate or impress the Word of God.

It is the Word of God that brings conviction of sin. "Is not my word like as a fire? saith the Lord; and like a hammer that breaketh the rock in pieces?" (Jer. 23:29).

It is the Word of God that brings light and understanding into the dark, deceitful heart of man: "For the Word of God is quick, and powerful, and sharper than any twoedged sword, piercing even to the dividing asunder of soul and spirit, and of the joints and marrow, and is a discerner of the thoughts and intents of the heart" (Heb. 4:12).

It is the Word of God that is used by the Holy Spirit in effecting in the human heart the new birth: "Being born again, not of corruptible seed, but of incorruptible, by the Word of God, which liveth and abideth for ever" (1 Pet. 1:23).

The unbeliever searches and sighs, "Oh, I wish I could believe. I wish I did have saving faith. I wish I knew how to trust Him!" Well, there is only one way to get faith. Here it is: "Faith cometh by hearing, and hearing by the Word of God" (Rom. 10:17). You see, faith does not come by looking for it, praying for it, striving for it, hoping for it; you hear the Word of God say, "But as many as received Him to them gave He power to become the sons of God, even to them that believe on His name" (Jn. 1:12). You accept His Word; you believe that God's record concerning you, a sinner, and concerning His Son, a Savior, is true; you take God at His Word. Thus you have heard the Word, and thereby faith in Christ as your own Savior spontaneously rises, and you exclaim, "He is mine forever more; I know whom I have believed!"

Evangelist *Alexander Stewart* tells how, before his conversion, Christians quoted Scripture to him and urged him that all he had to do for Salvation was to take God at His Word and believe in the Lord Jesus Christ as Savior. But he thought that was far too easy. He went about it according to his own idea—he joined a church, sang in the choir, and became quite a worker. He hoped in all these things to obtain peace with God; but there was no peace.

One day, while he was reading in his Bible the parable of the sower, he came to the words, "Then cometh the devil, and taketh away the Word out of their hearts, lest they should believe and be saved." Stewart put down his Bible and exclaimed, "Will you look at that! Even the devil knows that they will be saved if they take God at His Word and believe." That day he settled it by turning to Christ and trusting Him as Savior.

It is the Word of God that gives assurance of salvation: "These things have I written unto you that believe on the name of the Son of God; that ye may know that ye have eternal life, and that ye may believe on the name of the Son of God" (1 Jn. 5:13). A few minutes ago, the door bell rang. It was our yard man. "Are you saved?" I said to him after the greeting and a few words leading up to it. He waited a moment. I could see he was moved. "Yes, Sir, I is saved," he said emphatically. "You seem to be quite sure," I replied; "how do you know you are?"

"Well, I know I am saved because I love the brethren."

"That's fine evidence," I answered again. "What did you do to be saved?"

"I trusted Christ as my personal Savior. None other died for me."

"Who told you that you would be saved if you accepted Christ?" I asked finally.

In a spirited voice, he shot back at me instantly, "Well, that's what the Book tells me." And he started to quote Scripture to substantiate the reason for the hope that is within him.

"That's authority enough," I said. "You need no more."

Divine energy for salvation and for sanctification resides in the Word of God. Let us make sure to scatter and to water that precious seed into all kinds of soil. "The sower leaves his couch to go forth into the frosty air and tread the heavy soil; and as he goes he weeps because of past failures, or because the ground is so sterile, or the weather so unseasonable, or his corn so scarce, and his enemies so plentiful and so eager to rob him of his reward. He drops a seed and a fear, a seed and a tear, and so goes on his way. In his basket he has seed which is precious to him, for he has little of it, and it is his hope for the next year. Each grain leaves his hand with anxious prayer that it may not be lost: he thinks little of himself, but much of his seed, and he eagerly asks, 'Will it prosper? Shall I receive a reward for my labour?'" (*C. H. Spurgeon*).

In the morning sow thy seed, nor stay thy hand at evening hour,
Never asking which shall prosper—both may yield thee fruit and flower:
Thou shalt reap of that thou sowest; though thy grain be small and bare,
God shall clothe it as He pleases, for the harvest full and fair;
Though it sink in turbid waters, hidden from thy yearning sight,
It shall spring in strength and beauty, ripening in celestial light;
Ever springing, ever ripening;—not alone in earthly soil,
Not alone among the shadows, where the weary workers toil;
Gracious first-fruits there may meet thee of the reaping-time begun;—
But upon the Hill of Zion, 'neath the Uncreated Sun,
First the *fulness* of the blessing shall the faithful laborer see,
Gathering fruit to life eternal, harvest of Eternity.*

—Frances Ridley Havergal

THE ABIDING ASSURANCE OF RESULTS

You are a wise man for sowing the precious seed, for "he that goeth forth and weepeth, bearing precious seed, shall doubtless come again . . . bringing his sheaves." *Doubtless* you will gather sheaves from your sowing. You will return to this field, not to sow, but to reap; not to weep, but to rejoice. The harvest is assured. God has promised blessing upon His own Word. "For as the rain cometh down, and the snow from heaven, and returneth not thither, but watereth the earth, and

---

* Taken from "Poems" by Frances Ridley Havergal. Used by permission of E. P. Dutton & Co., Inc., New York.

maketh it bring forth and bud, that it may give seed to the sower, and bread to the eater: so shall My Word be that goeth forth out of My mouth: it shall not return unto Me void, but it shall accomplish that which I please, and it shall prosper in the thing whereto I sent it" (Isa. 55:10, 11).

Some sinners never listen to the message of God's Word seriously. They are the Wayside soil. They are indifferent, unresponsive to the urging of the Holy Spirit. Satan takes the Word out before it has a chance to root.

Other sinners are more hardened in their own ways. The ground is rocky. The soil is shallow. The response is more superficial.

Then there are those who have good intentions about the things of God, but in whom the "cares of this world" and the "deceitfulness of riches" choke out the good seed and keep it from fruition. This is the soil where the thorns sprang up. They were preoccupied with the affairs of this life; they were distracted from that which the Spirit would do for them.

But, thank God, some seed falls in good soil, and it takes firm root, grows up and bears fruit a hundredfold.

Personal work can be done in many ways. The personal conversation, face to face, is undoubtedly the most effective. But you may also speak to people about their souls over the telephone and by means of correspondence. You may also win souls by persevering prayer. *Dr. Lewis Sperry Chafer* (1871-1952) has frequently made the discerning statement, "You may not be able to talk to the soul about the Lord, but you can always talk to the Lord about that soul." Pray for them regularly and believingly and perseveringly. Remember this, God is on your side when you pray for salvation of souls. He is not willing that any should perish.

Then there is the vast ministry of distributing attractive gospel tracts. We will never know until we are all gathered Home just how many souls have been snatched from the "burning" through the use of some tract that was handed out, followed by prayer. One of the best stories about the mighty stream of blessing a tract can cause is that of a tract that was given to *Richard Baxter* by an unknown man. Through its message Baxter became a believer. He wrote a book, *The Call to the Unconverted*, which led thousands to Christ. One of the converts was *Philip Doddridge*, whose work, *The Rise and Progress of Religion in the Soul*, was the means of turning other multitudes to Christ. One of these converts was *William Wilberforce*. He was the moving spirit in the abolition of slavery, helped found the British and Foreign Bible Society, and wrote the book, *A Practical View of Christianity,* which God used to the salvation of many. Among the converts was *Leigh Richmond*, whose tract, *The Dairyman's Daughter,* in turn, brought many more multitudes to Christ.

Be faithful in planting the precious seed! Water it with tears and prayers. God will bring forth a glorious harvest, not of golden corn, but of "precious stones."

THE INCENTIVE OF HOME-COMING

"He that goeth forth and weepeth, bearing precious seed, shall doubtless come again *with rejoicing*, bringing his sheaves *with him.*"

Toil on, scatter the precious seed and weep, because without any doubt in the world, you will go Home after a little while with joy unspeakable and full of glory. All those whom you have led to the Lord will forever be your "joy and crown."

All heaven is now intent upon this greatest business on earth—soul-winning—and is vibrant with joy when a soul is made a citizen of that eternal country. The shepherd finds the lost sheep, "he layeth it on his shoulders, rejoicing. And when he cometh home, he calleth together his friends and neighbors, saying unto them, Rejoice with me; for I have found my sheep which was lost" (Lu. 15:5, 6).

A woman seeks diligently for the piece of silver she lost, until she finds it. Then she calls together her friends and neighbors and says, "Rejoice with me; for I have found the piece which I had lost" (Lu. 15:9).

The prodigal son comes to himself, returns home, confesses his sin against heaven and against his father. The fatted calf is killed, the robe and ring and shoes adorn the son, and there is great rejoicing and feasting in the happy home; "for this my son was dead, and is alive again" (Lu. 15:11-24).

"I say unto you, that likewise joy shall be in heaven over one sinner that repenteth, more than over ninety and nine just persons, which need no repentance" (Lu. 15:7).

Home-coming day will soon be here for each of us, and we shall enter into the joy of the Lord and into the joy of harvest. There is no joy comparable to the soul-winner's joy. Even here on earth, despite our burdens and tears, we experience foretastes of that solid joy. There is no thrill on the face of the earth like that which shivers in your innermost being when you see the benign smile and the heavenly peace upon the face of the boy or girl whom you have just led to the Lord. When that young heart looks earnestly up to God and says, "Thank you, Lord, for saving my soul," you cannot contain yourself, your cup quickly overflows, you resolve again, "God, I have tasted the divine flavor of the believer's ripe fruit. Now nothing else can satisfy. All earthly joys are empty cisterns. All fame and honors and plaudits that Society of Hollywood or Governments can bestow are but as the grass of the field. God, the rest of my days I spend, the rest of my life's every resource I want spent in winning precious souls."

Indeed, this is joy abounding, but we shall drink more deeply above. Home-coming day will soon be here for each of us, and we shall then enter into the joy of the Lord, and into the joy of harvest. Your "labor is not in vain in the Lord." Some of the sheaves will have been gathered ahead of you, some you will bring with you, and yet more will follow you. Your lands, your houses, your wealth you will leave behind. Your fame, your earthly honors, your pins and ribbons and bars you will forsake here below. Only the souls you have won to Christ during your earthly pilgrimage will you be able to take with you.

You may safely build upon that foundation "precious stones."

Oh, what a Home-coming Day that will be!

Rev. A. B. Hunter, pastor of the Bible Presbyterian Church in Tacoma, Washington, who came to this continent from Mountinellick, Ireland, as a young man, relates a true incident which his mother witnessed in King's County, Ireland. In that community lived the Throng family. They had two daughters, Mary and Helen, who, though Christians and in the church, were worldly-minded, unspiritual, and the thought of winning souls scarcely ever even crossed their minds. They finished school and were mature young women, when Mary grew seriously ill and died.

Embalming regulations in those days were lax. Funeral arrangements were made. Mary Throng lay in the casket at the front of the church, loved ones and friends gathered in mourning, and the service was about to be concluded, when Mary sat up in the casket. Surprised and mystified, alarmed and over-joyed, the family rushed up to her. And after many exclamations and tears of rejoicing, the family said, "Tell us, Mary, what was it like; what can you recall?"

Apparently having been in a sound coma, Mary said, "It all seems like a strange dream. I found myself by a wide river where people were crossing in boats. They were coming there from all directions. Two or three or large groups were getting into each boat and rowing across the river. On the other side, I could see the Lord receiving them at the gates of glory. I looked for someone to come and get into my boat with me. I looked this way and that way, but no one came. So I got into the boat myself, and rowed across. The Lord greeted me, and pathetically asked me, 'Mary, did you not bring anyone with you? Go back then and bring someone with you.' At that point I awoke, and here I am."

> Must I go and empty-handed
> Must I meet my Savior so;
> Not one soul with which to greet Him,
> Must I empty-handed go?"

Let us be going forth, and weeping, bearing the precious seed!

Building "precious stones!" Wonderful! But let us remember that unless we build also "gold" and "silver," we will neither have the desire for long, nor have the qualifications for building the "precious stones."

—6—

Building Wood, Hay and Stubble

What is the course of the life
Of mortal men on earth?—
Most men eddy about
Here and there—eat and drink,
Chatter and love and hate,
Gather and squander, are raised
Aloft, and hurl'd in the dust,
Striving blindly, achieving
Nothing; and, then they die—
Perish—and no one asks
Who or what they have been,
More than he asks what waves
In the moonlit solitudes mild
Of the midmost Ocean have swelled,
Foam'd for a moment, and gone.

—*Matthew Arnold*

A Christian is a person who is resting for his salvation upon the foundation laid by God, which is Jesus Christ.

"Now if any man build upon this foundation gold, silver, precious stones, wood, hay, stubble" (1 Cor. 3:12).

The word "now," as used here, is continuative, implying that only those persons who are already established upon the foundation can build upon it gold, silver, precious stones, wood, hay, and stubble. It is essential to see this and to distinguish clearly as we proceed. You must first become a Christian before you can live a Christian life. You must first become God's child if you would walk as becometh a child of God. You must first be "born again" of the Spirit if you are to respond to the Spirit's directions in your everyday life. You cannot render unto God any service whatsoever, not even the "wood, hay, stubble" type, unless you have first of all become a recipient of eternal life as the gracious gift of God.

If you are God's child, through faith in the God-provided Savior, Jesus Christ, the pertinent question for you is: *Now* what are you building? What is the nature of your thoughts, your aspirations, your enjoyments? What is the quality of your words, your deeds, your every service? "But let every man take heed how he buildeth thereupon," the Apostle urged; and one has only to read on to see that he is not speaking of *how much*, or of the *how* in the method of the believer's service. Notice, "Every man's work shall be made manifest: for the day shall declare it, because it shall be revealed by fire; and the fire shall try every man's work of what sort it is" (1 Cor. 3:13). The quality, the motives, the *sort* of life and service are here scrutinized. We would say, then, "Let every man take heed *what* he buildeth thereupon."

You may build upon that foundation the most valuable materials, imperishable and eternal, depicted by the choice symbols, "gold, silver, precious stones." These suggest the very best, the very highest, the very noblest life and service. Verily, it is that which is "ordained" by God—His very best— that we should build for eternity.

Or you may build the cheap, perishable materials suggested by "wood, hay, stubble." "Wood" (the original, however, suggests "pieces of wood picked up here and there") can be fashioned into something beautiful and of some temporary value, but it will not stand the fire. "Hay" is of less worth than the wood, but has some value in giving nourishment. It is devoured by fire in a flash. "Stubble" suggests a life of less value still, and is utterly unworthy of a person who is called by Christ's Name.

It is for you to choose and to determine which you will build. No one is in any way limited. Neither money, nor position, nor capabilities are conditions that are involved in this decision. Be not deceived by mere outward appearance of things and the opinions of men. Remember that wood, hay, and stubble do excel in bulk. Have a resolute regard for the reality and permanency in spiritual things. Remember also that God looketh on the heart and rewardeth them who have an eye single for His glory.

Do not allow yourself to think that your life as a Christian can be divided into "watertight compartments," so that you can say, "This is part of my work for God, and that is not." If you are God's child, every detail of your life is sacred unto the Lord. In every bit of your life and at all times you are to be in His will, carrying out His holy purposes. "Whatsoever ye do in word or deed, do all in the name of the Lord Jesus, giving thanks to God and the Father by Him . . . whatsoever ye do, do it heartily, as to the Lord, and not unto men" (Col. 3:17, 23). Remember that everything you do—perishable stuff, or the imperishable materials—all is built upon the foundation!

Frequently I meet people who are pressed and limited by poverty; and others, enduring physical pain, are confined to room and bed; and often I hear them murmur discontent and say, "Well, it seems that my life is wasted. I cannot do much. I guess I have to resign myself to this humdrum existence." Not so, dear friend, a thousand times no. Your depriving circumstances may have put you in the most enviable position wherein you may build "gold, silver and precious stones."

Let us take heed that in all conditions and in all things we are "approving ourselves as the ministers of God, in much patience, in afflictions, in necessities, in distresses . . . by pureness, by knowledge, by longsuffering, by kindness, by the Holy Ghost, by love unfeigned . . . as sorrowful, yet alway rejoicing; as poor, yet making many rich; as having nothing, and yet possessing all things" (2 Cor. 6:4, 6, 10).

Exactly two weeks ago, I called on the dear lady who had to give up all her "church work" years ago because of arthritis and high blood pressure; but her devotion to the Lord, her discernment of the Word, and her lofty outlook upon the God-designed future were to my heart delightful spiritual tonic. The short time of fellowship with this much-tested saint was a heavenly benediction that still lingers. Her concern for the salvation of the lost was burning brightly. Obvious, isn't it? She is building much "gold, silver, precious stones."

She reminded me, in some respects, of the alabaster box of very precious spikenard which Mary of Bethany bought with the life's savings of her meager earnings in order to anoint the Lord's body. Fit expression of sweet devotion to her Lord and God. But Judas and others objected. I suppose they thought it would have been better if she had used that money to build some neighborhood park for children or endow some poor house. Christ Jesus silenced all objections, "She hath done what she could." Indeed, she had. She built pure "gold," and "wheresoever this gospel shall be preached throughout the whole world, this also that she hath done shall be spoken of for a memorial of her" (Mk. 14:3-9).

The familiar story of Cripple Tom, which I heard early in my Christian life, helped to bring out for me the matter of abiding Christian service into clear perspective. Tom, an orphan boy, made his living sweeping streets. Injured in a traffic accident, he was invalided for the rest of his days. He lived out his days in a tiny, third-story attic room on a narrow London street. Grouchy "Granny" half-waited on him. Few friends called on him. Tom was saved by reading the Bible he had bought with the money his best friend, Jack, had left him. Tom had constant communion with God, and his soul was burning with a passionate desire to reach others with the message of God. God answered his longing by giving him the thought of writing out verses of Scripture on pieces of paper and throwing them out on the street below. He would write out the verses that had meant the most to him, would pray that God's Spirit would accompany the Word, and then he'd let it fly out the window.

"Granny" complained about not being able to supply him with enough paper, so Tom asked her to cut down on his morning porridge and give him more paper. Wonderful blessing attended this lad's unusual ministry.

A country gentleman, who was spiritually revived through a verse of Scripture that lighted on his hat when he passed by on that street, offered to take Tom to an institution where he would be better taken care of, but Tom refused the offer on the grounds that the comforts might hinder him from carrying on his God-given ministry. Tom, too, did what he could. He built much "gold and silver, precious stones," despite his pinching circumstances. Great is his reward in heaven.

Here is another example of someone who felt that his circumstances forced him to build only "wood, hay, stubble." When a young man, he wanted to devote himself to full-time Christian service as a pastor or missionary. But he was the only wage-earner for his widowed mother and the rest of the family. He could not get away to go to college and Seminary to prepare himself for the special service. Toiling on steadily to provide for those loved ones, many times he may have felt something like this, "Well, I have missed my calling. I wanted to be God's servant in proclaiming the gospel, but I am forced to go on working in this office and living the matter-of-fact life."

Do not lose heart, dear friend. *"Thou didst well that it was in thine heart."* If it was sincerely and definitely in your heart to devote all your time to preaching the gospel, God, who seeth the heart, will give you the same reward as you would have earned if you had done it. Only keep an eye single for His glory in all that you do, and let not the hidden dishonesty of your heart in any way trip you up. "Thou didst well that it was in thine heart"— that is what God told David. You will remember it was David who purposed in his heart to build a suitable House of Worship for his Lord. He planned it. He gathered materials for it. But he died without building the house. His son, Solomon, arose in his place, and built a magnificent temple unto the Lord, at the dedication of which he said, "It was in the heart of David my father to build an house for the name of the Lord God of Israel. And the Lord said unto David my father, Whereas it was in thine heart to build an house unto my name, *thou didst well that it was in thine heart.* Nevertheless thou shalt not build the house" (1 Kgs. 8:17-19).

The purpose of David's heart was recognized, and for it he was rewarded. God looks on the motives, as well as the moves. He has more regard unto the spirit of our works than He does their appearance in the estimation of men. God not only sees that cup of cold water that you gave to the thirsty one, but also why you gave it, and in whose name and for whose credit you did it. Let's follow David up a little. Why was he so anxious to build the House for the Lord? Was it to advance his "denomination"? Was it to improve the appearance of his town? Or was it to impress his fellow-citizens that truly he was a very "religious" person? Foolish, though common, thoughts.

Here is the answer: "One thing have I desired of the Lord, that will I seek after; that I may dwell in the house of the Lord all the days of my life, to behold the beauty of the Lord, and to inquire in His temple" (Psa. 27:4). This was the ever-vibrating motive of his heart before his God. He felt that same concern for the spiritual welfare of others: "Give unto the Lord, O ye mighty, give unto the Lord glory and strength. Give unto the Lord the glory due unto His name; worship the Lord in the beauty of holiness" (Psa. 29:1, 2).

Those who are least seen and known for their good works, those who may be least favored to do so by material circumstances, those whose plans have been disturbed by sickness, by adversities and reverses—those oftentimes are building most effectively for the eternal glory of God, and for themselves an everlasting memorial.

BUILDING WOOD

On the other hand, it is verily happening before our eyes every day that those who are reverenced and lauded for their mighty works are in reality only building wood.

What is building "wood"? Let us consider it a moment. Wood possesses temporary value. It fills a need. It is very extensively used by all peoples everywhere. It can be made to look quite impressive.

It is, indeed, a fitting figure of that religious activity, so common in every generation, which busies itself with much ado outwardly, but which is seriously lacking in spiritual reality and power. This outward activity of the church, with its display of machinery and requirements, is so apt to reduce to a kind of insignificance the inward individual objective of life and service. The organization itself becomes the final purpose of life. The mission overtops and puts into the shade the spiritual realities and the purposes it was designed to propagate. We become anxious about the success of our society or church. We become absorbed with its successes and its machinery. We quickly lose sight of the Lord Jesus Christ, and, although we still preach Him and teach Him and reverence Him, our heart devotions are largely drawn into that which we are accomplishing. Therein our service becomes earthly and temporal.

Let no one be led to believe by these remarks that the church is thereby disparaged, and its noble mission minimized. No, indeed. The church-society is beautiful, and its mission is heavenly, but the machinery for it is very much like the machinery for anything else. Its leaders, its departments, its boards, its committees, its business, its advertising—all these, in the main, are like the machinery for any other concern. *Dr. J. B. Mozley* put it this way, "The church is undoubtedly in its design a spiritual society, but it is also a society of this world; and it depends upon the *inward motive* of a man whether it is to him a spiritual society or a worldly one."

When the individual becomes absorbed in a blind obedience to a denominational body, it corrupts the quality of his spiritual life and service, and ensnares the man into a kind of self-interest. He follows more resolutely "after the tradition of men . . . and not after Christ" (Col. 2:8). The work prospers outwardly. Members are added. Budgets are increased. New buildings are raised. The public is impressed. The individual becomes zealous for the sake of his growing enterprise. He becomes proud of his group, his school, his cause. In all this activity Christ is not excluded, but He is very seriously eclipsed. The eye is not single for His glory and His honor and His praise. The church to such an individual, obviously, has become a worldly society.

But follow a bit further. In such an atmosphere the divine message is quickly corrupted also. Witnessing and winning souls first becomes of a secondary nature, and soon after becomes only a thing for casual reference. The preacher finds more delight in discussing current topics than in preaching the Word. The elders are more concerned about adding members and raising budgets than they are about winning souls. The Sunday School teacher works feverishly to get the attendance banner, and when she gathers the bright, young faces about her, and one of those earnest lads asks her, "What must I do to be saved," she fumbles a little and then gives mouth to the Satanic delusion, "Be good, sonny, be good, and be faithful to the church, and you will be all right."

Yes, all that looks big in every way and has the semblance of a spiritual and lasting work. But, alas, it is far from being the real thing, and is well summarized by the Apostle in 2 Tim. 3:5, "Having a form of godliness, but denying the power thereof: from such turn away." Yes, building, and building much, but building only "wood."

The sphere of this religious activity gives the person considerable satisfaction and a remarkable prop to lean upon. It eases the conscience. It gains for that person recognition upon a high plane. The service gives the desired opportunity for the display of mental gifts, the boundless faith and the urgent zeal; and all these things interpret the person favorably in the estimation of the admiring public. The popular judgment sets them upon a high pedestal morally and religiously. It gets much praise of men.

But the person who engages in such service may object to this analysis of himself. He may say that this service does not exalt him directly or personally, as the Pharisee might have said when denounced by Christ for his proselytism: "I have no private gain in the propagation of the doctrines of my religion; it is no gain to me personally; I only devote myself to it because the extension of vital truth, or at least that which we believe to be such, is a solemn duty. I value my beliefs. I think they are important. This stirs me to want to impart it to others. We must be zealous in winning others to our sect. I belong to it. My forefathers belonged to it. If I didn't believe in it, I would quit and join some other. We must be zealous in making the creed and principles of our sect known to others. We are naturally glad when our efforts prosper."

Indeed, every Pharisee, then and now, makes some such defense for himself. But the grieved Lord, who sees the heart and all its motives, denounces this perverted spirit in unsparing terms. Eight times He uses the solemn expression, "Woe unto you." Seven times He calls them "hypocrites." Twice He speaks of them as "blind guides," twice as "fools and blind," once as "serpents and a generation of vipers."

Let us mark well the language of one or two of those scathing "woes": "Woe unto you, scribes and Pharisees, hypocrites! For ye compass sea and land to make one proselyte, and when he is made, ye make him twofold more the child of hell than yourselves. . .Woe unto you, scribes and Pharisees, hypocrites! For ye are like unto whited sepulchres, which indeed appear beautiful outward, but are within full of dead men's bones, and of all uncleanness. Even so ye also outwardly appear righteous unto men, but within ye are full of hypocrisy and iniquity" (Matt. 23:15, 27, 28).

Christ's stern judgment went beneath the surface and brought into the open all those hidden things of dishonesty and earthiness that so frequently animate the most religious workers. It all has foul smell. It is an abomination before the Lord. It is only "wood." Service, but dull as wood. Only creedal, sentimental, and ritualistic stuff. It has no abiding solidity, no lasting value, no permanent duration. And, irrespective of how impressive and fashionable and useful it may appear, it will be quickly reduced to ashes when the same Christ again, with His all-searching glance, evaluates our works.

BUILDING HAY

Let us now consider briefly those who are building hay.

What is building "hay"? Hay has less value than wood, and is more quickly devoured by fire. And yet, we must realize that it is intended to represent some form of so-called Christian service. It is built upon the foundation. The Apostle in those six symbols sets forth six qualities of life and service, beginning with "gold," the highest and best, and ending with "stubble," the most worthless. I have suggested that building "wood" symbolizes life and service which promote and glorify merely your church, your sect, your society. Then building "hay" indicates the service where the flesh plays the dominant part and where self seeks the preeminence.

One cannot contemplate Christendom of the present day without an indescribable feeling of sadness and heaviness. The tone of Christian discipleship is so excessively low, its aspect so sickly, and its spirit so exceedingly enfeebled. Surely the Apostle Paul was speaking of us when he said, "All seek their own, not the things which are Jesus Christ's" (Phil. 2:21). Much that is called Christian work is only a colorful effervescence of the flesh. Sometimes it is not even very colorful. When the men on the board indulge in a pretty hot campaign for the office of chairman or Sunday School Superintendent, the stirrings of the old flesh stand out in unvarnished hideousness. And when some good sister refuses to teach a Sunday School class because the class is small and would appear to be an insult to her superior ability and years of priority—when the flesh so powerfully displays its ugliness, I say, it is not even colorful. All such selfishness, under some clever cloak, or undisguised, is worthy of unmingled contempt.

We must guard vigilantly against the strivings of self-interest and self-exaltation, which constantly assert themselves. *Carlyle* said, "Always there is a black spot in our sunshine, it is ... the shadow of ourselves." Self is our mightiest antagonist. *Luther* once said that he was more afraid of the *self* pope than he was of the Roman pope. Pride likes to come out on parade—be assured that it has more than one change of clothes—and demands congratulations and applause. Self-conceit convinces its victim that his feelings have been hurt and urges him to go on a long pouting spell. Envy makes people say things and do things which undoubtedly have their origin in hell and are fanned by all manner of satanic influences.

All this littleness and selfishness and bickering is gross carnality and is despicable in the sight of God. "For ye are yet carnal: for whereas there is among you envying, and strife, and divisions, are ye not carnal, and walk as men?" (1 Cor. 3:3). At the bottom of most splits and divisions is old king self, subtly working out through some "Diotrephes, who loveth to have the preeminence among them" (3 Jn. 9). Secretly all such people seem to have higher regard for the opinions and applause of men than they do for the blessed will and approval of God. They do things to be noticed by people. They are swayed by public opinion, just as the hay is by every wind and every breeze.

Sad and tragic is the lot of all such. They are wastefully burning themselves out, and building only "hay." Perishable stuff. It is of the earth, earthy. It has no abiding spiritual character. It has mind in it, energy in it, individuality in it, but not Christ in it, and Christ wholly. It uses Christ only to advance itself before men. All work which glorifies only the worker must perish. Only the work which glorifies Christ can stand the fire-test. How exceedingly cautious we must be. How closely we must test our own work in God's sight to make sure that no self-seeking has crept into it. "If we would judge ourselves, we should not be judged" (1 Cor. 11:31).

And finally let us glance at the most worthless life and service—building stubble.

BUILDING STUBBLE

And what is building "stubble"? Well, here is a Christian who on every hand is compromising with the world. He thinks he can be more effective if he is sociable with the worldlings, flexible enough to share in their habits, and broad-minded enough to take in their pleasures. He gives himself all such liberties which make him a jolly-good-fellow, a "cultured Christian," popular with the worldly crowd. He qualifies for any situation. He thinks he is actually doing great things, because he is in great demand with the clubs and the parties, and realizes not, poor fellow, that he is selling out his spiritual birthright for a mess of flimsy pottage.

He is like the eagle of a certain species, which is bold enough to attack the seal. It fixes its claws quickly in the seal's flesh, and, by the strength of its wings, frequently manages to pull the seal ashore. But more frequently, the seal is too strong for the eagle, and, not being able to let go its hold, the eagle is dragged down into the deep and drowned.

What happens to the Christians who give themselves the license to associate freely with the worldly? In the first place, they lose their testimony. They are submerged into the sea of worldly wisdom and worldly ways. They lose their savor. They have no power with God, and, consequently, they have no spiritual influence upon those with whom they associate.

They have taken the bit in their teeth and dared deliberately to disobey God by currying favor and fellowship with the Egyptians. Wherein have they disobeyed God? Listen to the express instruction of God, dear heart, "Be ye not unequally yoked together with unbelievers: for what fellowship hath righteousness with unrighteousness? And what communion hath light with darkness? And what concord hath Christ with Belial? Or what part hath he that believeth with an infidel? And what agreement hath the temple of God with idols? For ye are the temple of the living God; as God hath said, I will dwell in them, and walk in them; and I will be their God, and they shall be my people. Wherefore come out from among them, and be ye separate, saith the Lord, and touch not the unclean thing; and I will receive you, and will be a Father unto you, and ye shall be My sons and daughters, saith the Lord Almighty" (2 Cor. 6:14-18).

This is not some man's opinion. This is the will of God for every believer. You cannot please God and walk hand in hand with the world. You cannot witness for Christ and break His heart by courting darkness at the same time. You cannot have fellowship with darkness and at the same time reprove and rebuke their ways. You cannot grieve the Holy Spirit and at the same time witness in the power of the Holy Spirit so as to convince them of their sin. It simply does not work. A few days ago, I heard from the lips of a radiant girl, who is making remarkable strides in her Christian life, "I know it doesn't work, because I've tried it. I used to go to dances and theatres and at the same time try to teach a Sunday School class. I knew that one of the two had to go—either my class, or the dance and theatre. It simply did not work. I had no desire to win souls to Christ. I had very little love in my heart for Christ." How true! How true!

A believer who defiles himself with the besmirching things of the world, and is absorbed in the unfruitful works of darkness, has neither the blessing of God nor the love of God in him. Does not God say expressly, "Love not the world, neither the things that are in the world. If any man love the world, the love of the Father is not in him. For all that is in the world, the lust of the flesh, and the lust of the eyes, and the pride of life, is not of the Father, but is of the world. And the world passeth away, and the lust thereof: but he that doeth the will of God abideth for ever." (1 Jn. 2:15-17). The person who will stubbornly disobey such explicit instructions will some day suddenly and surely come to a tragic end, as did Belshazzar, who dared to defile in a riotous feast the vessels of gold and silver set apart for sacred uses in the temple of Jerusalem.

And yet, in the face of such clear revelation of the will of God for His own, one sees on every hand good people, Christian people, who apparently know the Word, preferring the "husks" of Satan to the "abundant life" of the Good Shepherd. Only last night I was told about the splendid minister, who knows and preaches the Bible to his congregation, who is bringing up his daughters in a "normal way." He allows them to go to dances (well-escorted, of course), to picture shows (well-chosen ones only); he allows them to belong to the sororities, etc.,—all of this so that they may have a "normal" bringing up. I am quite sure that the world calls that "normal." Spiritual believers, however, call that positively "sub-normal."

One wishes, in all such instances, to press home one or two questions: "Are you pleasing the Lord by doing that? Does it help you to win souls? Does it develop your spiritual life?" Such questions silence all their arguments.

Consider, dear friends, the solid advice of Paul, which speaketh volumes to those who would be spiritual and who would grow in the graces of the Spirit: "And this I pray, that your love may abound yet more and more in knowledge and in all judgment; that ye may approve things that are excellent; that ye may be sincere and without offence till the day of Christ; being filled with the fruits of righteousness, which are by Jesus Christ, unto the glory and praise of God" (Phil. 1:9-11).

May the Lord be pleased to give you that fuller knowledge of spiritual things and that closer discernment of values, so that you may in all sincerity choose for yourself not just that which is right, but high above that, those things which are excellent—God's best for you. May you have a flaming passion to "press toward the mark for the prize of the high calling of God in Christ Jesus" (Phil. 3:14).

You are God's child. You have only one life. *Each moment* of every day you are building something upon that foundation. Let every one take heed what he buildeth thereupon! Which is it—

> "Stubble," or "precious stones,"
> "hay," or "silver,"
> "wood," or "gold"?

-7-

The Fiery Test

Each morning the memorizers and counsellors attending our camps some years ago, assembled reverently among the stately pines which seemed urgently to point the earnest-hearted youth heavenward. The shimmering lake beside us seemed also to reflect His glory. To illustrate these "Morning Watch" messages, taken from 1 Corinthians 3, an interesting and effective object lesson was devised, which was progressively added to with the development of the messages each morning.

The first morning, I laid on the ground a big concrete slab, painted in deep red. This, I said, represents the foundation which God has laid. "For other foundation can no man lay than that is laid, which is Jesus Christ." The first three chapters of this book record some of the thoughts that were used in showing them that there is positively no other ground for our redemption apart from the finished work of Jesus Christ in His death and resurrection for our sins. Then I asked them if they could tell me what I could do to get myself upon that concrete slab. "Just simply step on it," came the reply in chorus with a slight tone of disgust that I would even wonder how it could be done. So very simple, isn't it? And that is the only part that you can play in your salvation. Simply take the step of faith in the Savior, Christ Jesus. Rest forever your soul's salvation upon Him. There is no other way.

The next day, I built upon the foundation several rounds of brick, which were painted gold. "Let every man take heed *what* he buildeth thereupon." "Now if any man build upon this foundation gold . . ." This is the greatest thing you can do for God. Only remember that you cannot do anything for Him, not even give a cup of cold water to another in His Name, unless you are first established upon that foundation. You must be saved yourself before you can serve Him. Commune intimately and personally with your God—this is building "gold."

The next morning, I laid upon the gold bricks several rounds of brick painted silver. This indicates the fellowship of believers about the things of God—enjoying together and witnessing together and suffering together and exalting together Him, whom we love.

The following morning, I laid about the top of the silver bricks variously shaped stones and rocks of different sizes; these I had painted in brilliant colors. Winning souls is building "precious stones." They that lead souls to Christ will shine with divine brilliance in heaven forever.

But the Scripture says that some build upon that foundation "wood, hay, stubble." That morning, I asked a group of young people to help me build upon the foundation. They were eager to do so. Would you like to gather for me small pieces of wood, some nice hay, and good stubble? They went forth enthusiastically. It's easy, you know, to build wood, hay, and stubble. To build gold, silver, and precious stones I rose early each day and worked at it quite industriously. And so here they come with lots of wood, hay, and stubble. "Wood" signifies that "religious" activity which looks impressive enough outwardly, but which lacks in spiritual reality and power. "Hay" suggests that service where the flesh plays the dominant part. "Stubble," the most worthless of all, is that Christian who thinks it expedient to compromise with the world in his walk and manner of life.

My object lesson was built somewhat in the form of a chimney, with an opening on the bottom of the back side for the draft. They enthusiastically loaded the wood, hay, and stubble into the "chimney."

Now, our works, as believers, shall be tested. We shall find out the quality and value of our Christian life and our service. "Every man's work shall be made manifest: for the day shall declare it, because it shall be revealed by fire; and the fire shall try every man's work of what sort it is (1 Cor. 3:13). BY FIRE! All right, we will apply the test. I struck a match, and applied it. A pall of heavy smoke rose through all the trash. High, lusty flames broke through and soon enveloped the wood, hay, and stubble. THERE GOES YOUR WHOLE LIFE, I shouted to them while the flames roared. COME AND SEE YE WHO BUILT WOOD, HAY, AND STUBBLE! Come and see what remains. They came and peered inside with tragic looks upon their faces. Ashes and the smell of smoke was all that remained.

BUT LOOK, the gold, the silver, and the precious stones remain. They, too, were tested. The flames searched and tested them also. But they abide.

The whole audience was subdued and silent. The effect was tremendous.

FIERY TEST

And all believers may well meditate upon and consider with "fear and trembling" this fiery test which every saint will surely pass through. "Every man's work shall be made manifest . . . the fire shall try every man's work of what sort it is." Yes, *every man's work.* This takes in every one who is resting upon the foundation, Christ Jesus, for his redemption.

The test shall be "by fire." This indicates that the test is to be definite, discriminating, decisive. It is sharper than the sharpest two-edged sword. Not only does it have a keenness of edge to pierce, but likewise it has the power to reveal and to bring completely into the open. This test of fire shall be thorough, searching, and perfectly efficient.

The elemental fire is an appropriate outward symbol of the all-searching judgment of God to which all our works shall be subjected in that Day. As fire does, so does God, in the end, thoroughly search out and reveal the true nature of all that we have wrought, and all but that which has abiding eternal quality will be utterly destroyed. Fire fairly represents the deeply penetrating power of God—the God concerning whom Moses of old said, "For the Lord thy God is a consuming fire" (Deut. 4:24). Such is the nature of the living God who will probe the secrets of all we have thought and done. He Himself saith, "I the Lord search the heart, I try the reins, even to give every man according...to the fruit of his doings" (Jer. 17:10).

"Every man's work shall be made manifest: for the day shall declare it." This refers to the final testing of the believer's works when *the* day, the great day for the Church, will come. "The day shall declare it," as it is, not as it has been thought to be. Now our works may look well, but, oh, what then? "But who may abide the day of His coming? And who shall stand when He appeareth? For He is like a refiner's fire, and like fullers' soap: and He shall sit as a refiner and purifier of silver: and he shall purify the sons of Levi, and purge them as gold and silver, that they may offer unto the Lord an offering in righteousness" (Mal. 3:2, 3).

One aspect of the outcome of Christ's coming to earth, is to prepare and purify the heavenly priesthood of believers, and "to purge them as gold and silver," so that the believers' life and works may indeed be "unto the Lord an offering in righteousness."

His coming also has another aspect—a darker one—which is related by the same prophet, "For, behold, the day cometh, that shall burn as an oven; and all the proud, yea, and all that do wickedly, shall be stubble: and the day that cometh shall burn them up, saith the Lord of hosts" (4:1). This refers, of course, to final judgment of the wicked; no saved person will be at that judgment. However, it is an accurate picture of what will happen to the works of those believers who built only "wood, hay, stubble." If the *proud* and the workers of *iniquity* are reckoned as stubble, so also are the works of the proud, self-seeking Christians. All their works will be consumed as in "an oven."

Herein is the twofold aspect of that test, that day, that judgment—to reveal the purified gold, an offering in righteousness unto the Lord, and to consume as in "an oven" the fruitless works of the flesh.

It was for such judgment that Christ came into the world at first (Isa. 10:17; Matt. 3:11, 12). God has so designed it that through Christ this judicial function shall be finally and completely fulfilled in the last day. "Because He hath appointed a day, in the which He will judge the world in righteousness by that Man whom He hath ordained" (Acts 17:31). Thus we see that this fiery testing of the believers' works will be accomplished through Christ.

And the Scripture speaks to us on this subject specifically, "For we must all appear before the judgment seat of Christ; that every one may receive the things done in his body, according to that he hath done, whether it be good or bad" (2 Cor. 5:10). "We" must all appear. This refers to all the believers. "Therefore judge nothing before the time, until the Lord come, who will bring to light the hidden things of darkness, and will make manifest the counsels of the hearts; and then shall every man have praise of God" (1 Cor. 4:5). Let every man take heed. Be not deceived.

"The day shall declare it." Live, serve, build with one eye

ever upon that *day*, when the "fire shall try every man's work of what sort it is." In a moment, in the twinkling of an eye the curtain may be drawn, the day will dawn, with a shout Christ will appear, and we shall ascend to meet Him in the air, and all stand before Him, whom the aged Apostle John envisioned from Patmos: "His head and His hairs were white like wool, as white as snow; and His eyes were as a flame of fire; and His feet like unto fine brass, as if they burned in a furnace; and His voice as the sound of many waters" (Rev. 1:14, 15).

Just one glance from the Savior, Jesus Christ—just one searching gaze of those eyes, "like a flame of fire," and the fiery test is on.

THE PURPOSE OF THE TEST

But let us keep clearly in mind the purpose of the test.

This may be briefly summarized in four statements—one negative and three positive. The purpose of the fiery test is *not* to determine whether or not you are saved and qualify for heaven. It is rather to manifest the basis of your service, and to reveal the real quality of that service.

You are redeemed by the work of Christ, who before the foundation of the world was determined to be your Savior, whose precious blood was spilt for you on this earth, and in whose atoning death and victorious resurrection you may confidently affix your faith and hope (1 Pet. 1:18-23). You are saved from sin's penalty forever by the grace of God (Eph. 2:8), and, dear friend, grasp this also, you are forever "kept by the power of God through faith unto salvation ready to be revealed in the last time" (1 Pet. 1:5). The purpose of the fiery test at the Judgment seat of Christ is not to determine whether or not you are saved. That was eternally determined for you when you reckoned upon the earth with the Lord and trustingly received Him as your own personal Savior.

After you were saved, you built upon that foundation— well, either for His glory, "gold, silver, precious stones"; or in the energy of the flesh you stacked up only "wood, hay, stubble."

Which is it? That is, expressly, the purpose of the test of fire: "to make manifest"; to "declare" it—reveal it; to "try" it—test it out.

First, to determine the basis on which your works rest. Already, Scripture tells us, the foundation of our redemption has been "tried" and found to be a "precious stone, a sure foundation" (Isa. 28:16). How, then, is our life's work related to Christ. He alone can be the source of all true saintliness of character and righteousness of life. He alone can breathe into our service divine energy an abiding value. Is not our service to be wrought also by faith in Christ?

What else could the Apostle Paul have meant when he said to the Galatians, "I am crucified with Christ: nevertheless I live; yet not I, but Christ liveth in me: and the life which I now live in the flesh I live by the faith of the Son of God, who loved me, and gave Himself for me" (2:20)? His own abilities, his own heritage, his own religious background, his own training, his own staunch character, his own zeal, his own blameless righteousness according to the law—all these he counted but as refuse, "that," as he wrote the believers at Philippi, "I may win Christ, and be found in Him, not having mine own righteousness, which is of the law, but that which is through the faith of Christ, the righteousness which is of God by faith" (3:8, 9).

Indeed, indeed, only as our souls are "rooted and grounded in Him," only as we move forward by faith in Him, can we build upon the foundation any fabric which will stand the searching test of that day.

Second, the test shall search out the spirit that inspired your service. All error, all falsehood, all unreality shall be instantly stripped away. The fiery ordeal will reveal whether the life has been animated and guided by a worldly, selfish spirit, or by a genuine desire to show forth the excellencies of the blessed, triune God.

I have an interesting clipping from an old Victorian magazine.

It is entitled, "The Worker's Dream." During the time of a spiritual awakening, a minister fell asleep in a chair. He dreamed that he saw a man coming to him with weights and measures and chemical apparatus, who said to him, "I want to analyze your zeal." The minister was very much pleased at this, believing that his zeal was great. The stranger used his scales and chemicals and recorded his findings as follows:

Weight in mass—One hundred pounds

Your life and zeal weighed out as follows.

Bigotry	10 parts
Personal ambition	23 parts
Love of praise	19 parts
Pride of church and denomination	15 parts
Pride of talent	14 parts
Love of authority	11 parts
Love to God	4 parts
Love to man	3 parts
Total.................................	100 parts - one hundred pounds

The minister awoke and cried out, "Lord, forgive me, the record is true!"

The mere form of our work, the place and space that it has visibly occupied on the stage of the world's history is of comparatively small importance. The spirit that has impelled it is what gives the work its living substance and its essential quality.

This brings us to the third positive aspect as to the purpose of the judgment of the believer's works—that is, to reveal the real quality of that service. Three symbols speak of service that is incombustible. It will endure the fire, and its abiding character will be only served by the fire to shine forth in its true worth. Indeed, it is not likely that *all* the works of the best and wisest of men will endure the revealing light and consuming fire of that test; but some of it will approve itself to God and stand the final test. Undoubtedly, this will be the work done in the divine strength, and deliberately for the glory of God. The "gold," the "silver," and the "precious stones" will glow with indescribable heavenly luster when the test is applied.

The three other symbols describe works which are combustible. The fire consumes them. The character of their works is more like those of the minister who saw himself analyzed in the dream. Pride, self-interest, and worldliness largely make up their bulk. They are only as the grass, whose glory fades even in time. They perish instantly when exposed to the test of the eternal. They have no abiding character. The searchlight of the DAY has "declared" them; the FIRE revealed what S-O-R-T they are.

London's prolific writer and compiler, *Hy Pickering*, tells the story of a professor who was showing to his friends various experiments with the Roentgen, or X-rays. Many beautifully dressed ladies were present, wearing, to all appearance, most rare and costly jewelry. Said the professor, "It is really wonderful the effect these rays have upon diamonds." So, lowering the lights in the room, he turned the X-rays on the sparkling gems which the ladies wore. Immediately the real diamonds flashed in all their full brilliancy; but alas, the beautiful paste imitation diamonds had lost all their luster. The X-rays discovered which were *real* and which were *imitation*, much to the dismay of some of the ladies present.

THE ISSUES, THE RESULTS

What will be the issues, the results when the all-searching X-rays of the all-seeing eye of the Almighty are turned upon our lives and our works in the pure light of heaven? That divine "fire," like some powerful alchemy, can elicit and extract every falsehood, and develop and reveal what is sterling and sincere and godly in man.

The unsaved will not be there. They will continue their profitless and darksome existence upon the earth. The graves of the peoples who died without Christ will continue undisturbed. The ashes of their bodies will remain in the earth. Their spirits will continue their tormenting imprisonment in the confines of Hades.

Now, back to the believers in Christ. They will all be present at the Judgment seat of Christ, those who died "in Christ," and whose redeemed spirits will inhabit their new bodies, glorified and incorruptible. Those who were translated into immortality without seeing physical death will also all be gathered about the Lord. Excitedly, all will await the result of the fiery test. The nature of those results is already given us.

"If any man's work shall be burned, he shall suffer loss: but he himself shall be saved; yet so as by fire" (1 Cor. 3:15). The "wood, hay, stubble" which they zealously built is consumed in a moment, and therein they "suffer loss," but they themselves are saved, "yet so as by fire," that is, barely—just saved and no more. Their works perish; but their salvation abides.

A life-work destroyed in a moment. A life lived and no fruit. No "well-done" from the Master, because all has been "ill-done." All because of self-reliance, self-interest, carelessness, sluggishness, and inattention to the revealed will of God.

These are like the man who goes to great pains to build for himself a beautiful house. One night it catches fire. He is suddenly awakened out of sound sleep to find the flames madly licking up the walls. His time is gone. He leaps out the window, and witnesses sadly his beautiful house and all his cherished personal belongings devoured by the uncompromising flames. That is exactly the way it will be with many Christians. Their energies and their time wasted! Their testimony lost! All their life lived for nothing! Yet, the believer himself will be saved. He will go to heaven.

Lot, in the Old Testament, is a good example of such a believer. He spent his precious years in the wicked city of Sodom. At first he located himself on the outskirts. Gradually he compromised with the Sodomites, grew in reputation, until he became one of the city fathers. His wife was simply charmed by the "high life" in Sodom. Their daughters naturally fell in "love" with Sodom's handsome men. We are told how "that righteous man dwelling among them . . . vexed his righteous soul from day to day with their unlawful deeds" (2 Pet. 2:8). He "vexed" his soul in that famous Vanity Fair, long since buried beneath brimstone, but he could not "sell out" his soul. It belonged to God. The decisive moment was approaching. God's messengers came, and almost had to pull Lot and his family out by their collars. They didn't want to leave. Poor Mrs. Lot was so attached to that sinful city that she became enshrined in a pillar of salt on the edge of that city. Then God destroyed Sodom with fire, and Lot was "saved so as by fire." Everything he lived for, everything he built was lost in a moment. His labors were lost. He himself was saved.

Sad, indeed, will be that day for all whose life's works will be speedily consumed.

But there is another group present. Their works withstood the Refiner's heat. Their works "abide." As a result of that test, no work will be made to appear better than it actually is; even so, none will be made to appear worse. Those many calm hours devoted to communing with the blessed God wrought upon the foundation imperishable stuff— "gold." The searching eye of the Judge in that Day will relieve it of any dross that may remain. The "gold" will radiate something of the light and glory and excellency of the Great God Himself. And the sterling qualities of "silver" (tempered by life's many trials as believers influenced each other heavenward by true spiritual companionship) will then be fully revealed. The souls whom you led to Christ are all there— "precious stones!" Oh, what rejoicing! Someone has whispered it around that the Lord has for you some special crown, adorned with many brilliant stones. But another has found out that He has scheduled for His own innumerable surprises, all of which are to manifest the exceeding riches of His grace. But hush, the time is not yet.

What a difference! Being saved "so as by fire" is in striking contrast to the "abundant entrance." May we strive earnestly for the ecstatic joy of the latter—that holy gladness which comes from seeing that we have not "lived in vain."

The curtain has not yet been drawn. The day has not dawned. The solemn, penetrating gaze is not yet. The verdicts of that pure white tribunal are guarded still, but we surely can see the finger pointing which seems to indicate—"Beyond, in this direction, behind this veil, things are different from what you are used to—everything will stand out in its proper character; everyone will be aboundingly rewarded according to his works."

When I stand at the judgment seat of Christ,
And He shows me His plan for me,
The plan of my life as it might have been
Had He had His way, and I see

How I blocked Him here, and I checked Him there
And I would not yield my will—
Will there be grief in my Savior's eyes,
Grief, though He loves me still?

He would have me rich, and I stand there poor,
Stripped of all but His grace,
While memory runs like a hunted thing
Down the paths I cannot retrace.

Then my desolate heart will well-nigh break
With the tears that I cannot shed;
I shall cover my face with my empty hands,
I shall bow my uncrowned head.

Lord, of the years that are left to me,
I give them to Thy hand;
Take me and break me, mold me to
The pattern Thou hast planned!

—*Martha Snell Nicholson*

~8~

The Glory of Rewards

It is not for a sign we are watching . . .
It is not for a Day we are looking . . .
It is not for a King we are longing . . .
It is not for a Judge . . .
For they are but adjuncts of Him . . .
We wait for the Lord, our Beloved,
Our Comforter, Master, and Friend,
The substance of all that we hope for,
Beginning of faith and its end.
We watch for our Savior and Bridegroom,
Who loved us and made us His own;
For Him we are looking and longing;
*For Jesus, and Jesus alone.**

—*Annie Johnson Flint*

"If any man's work abide which he hath built thereupon, he shall receive a reward" (1 Cor. 3:14). "And every man shall receive his own reward according to his own labour" (1 Cor. 3:8).

The person whose work was speedily consumed by the fiery test "shall suffer loss," yet he himself shall be saved, "so as by fire." Saved, but no rewards. To the one whose work shall pass the divine test and "abide," a reward shall be given.

---

* Copyright. Reprinted, by special permission, Evangelical Publishers, Toronto, Canada.

Do not confuse salvation and rewards. They are two distinct things. Forgiveness of sins, salvation, and eternal life can never be earned by any of our own works. They are the undeserved, unmerited gift of God to all who definitely and sincerely accept the Lord Jesus Christ as Savior and Lord (Rom. 6:23; Eph. 2:8, 9; Titus 3:5). After a person becomes a Christian, the work which he does in Jesus' Name and for His glory, and which will pass the probing of God's searchlight—work which will "abide" shall be rewarded.

Salvation is received strictly as a gift. Eternal life in heaven is a gift. But the rewards are earned. The reward is not for being on the Foundation, but for what is built thereon. Furthermore, note *Dr. C. I. Scofield's* concise distinction of these two things: "Salvation is a present possession (Lu. 7:50; Jn. 3:36; 5:24; 6:47), while rewards are a future attainment, to be given at the coming of the Lord (Matt. 16:27; 2 Tim. 4:8; Rev. 22:12)."

The goal is set, the immortal prize is before you. "So run, that ye may obtain" (1 Cor. 9:24). "Lay aside every weight, and the sin which doth so easily beset us, and let us run with patience the race that is set before us, looking unto Jesus the author and finisher of our faith" (Heb. 12:1, 2). Track-runners, prize fighters, and athletes discipline themselves most cautiously about their diet, their habits, and their rest, and assiduously apply themselves to vigorous exercise and training. They will permit no handicaps. They are "temperate in all things." They must be absolutely fit. And all that preparation simply to be able successfully to dash ahead of the others in track, or effectively to bash in another fellow's nose—and thereby win the corruptible crown.

How much more cautious should we be in making "no provision for the lust of the flesh," in keeping our "bodies in subjection," and in "bringing into captivity every thought to the obedience of Christ," so that we may run the race of life successfully, be approved of our Lord, and gain a crown incorruptible. Every sin is really besetting. Every weight is a hindrance. The devil would place these crooked thieves about us so that they might steal and bury away our heavenly treasures.

Nana Sahib, after he had lost his last battle in India, fell back into the jungles of Iheri—jungles so full of malaria that no mortal can live there. He carried with him also a ruby of remarkable luster and of great value. He died in those jungles; his body was never found, and the ruby has never been recovered.

Do not so foolishly and so wastefully with the prize that may be yours. "Look to yourselves, that we lose not those things which we have wrought, but that we receive a full reward" (2 Jn. 8).

"No man that warreth entangleth himself with the affairs of this life; that he may please him who hath chosen him to be a soldier. And if a man also strive for masteries, yet is he not crowned, except he strive lawfully" (2 Tim. 2:4, 5). The lustrous garland hangs over the goal, but "a man is not crowned unless he strives according to the laws" of the arena. The laws in the spiritual arena are two: No man can enter for the conflict except by faith in Christ as Savior; no man can win in the struggle but by diligent effort.

The first law is, "Believe on the Lord Jesus Christ." The second law is "Hold that fast which thou hast, that no man take thy crown" (Rev. 3:11). Keep the rules in mind, keep eternity for your background, and press on toward the mark for the prize.

We cannot now fully comprehend the meaning and the value of that prize. We only know that the prophets, the Apostles, and all the faithful servants of God had profound respect unto the recompense of that reward, and were remarkably stimulated at the very thought of it. The rewards are usually given according to the riches and dignity and interest of the rewarder. The Supreme Giver of good and perfect gifts is the Rewarder in this case. All things were made by Him. He inhabiteth eternity. "Knowing that of the Lord ye shall receive the reward of the inheritance: for ye serve the Lord Christ" (Col. 3:24). And this God is your Father. The Father knoweth how to give good gifts. "Thy Father which seeth in secret Himself shall reward thee openly" (Matt. 6:4). We may rest assured, then, that the rewards which God gives to the victors will be valuable and such as are well worth striving for with all our might.

Most people seem to make the "corruptible crown" the object of their fond ambitions. How many there are who are anxiously striving to gain the crown of fame! They are possessed with an insatiable craving to be recognized, to be esteemed, to be influential, to be remembered. There are others who seek to win the crown of wealth. Money is their chief concern. Always they are feverishly striving to make more money. Every standard is measured by money. Every value is reckoned in money. And to spur on these ambitions the world looks upon them with benign approval. These are the kinds of crowns that the world admires and applauds. But when they have won these crowns, what do they have but corruptible crowns, which actually bring little satisfaction to the winners, and which disintegrate with time. Poor disillusioned folk, in whose hands the years leave but the poorest things of life—withered leaves, faded flowers, straw, and bits of worthless tinsel!

But the rewards that our heavenly Father proffers us are satisfying, and such as will bring for us an "eternal weight of glory" (2 Cor. 4:17). They are to be rightfully and healthily coveted. All that talk about it being selfishness and unworthy for a Christian to be lured into richer service by the expectation of reward is just so much cant. The glorious expectation of rewards is one of the things that makes the Christian life reasonable—the sacrifices and sufferings in His Name bring great gain. The question was asked long ago, "Doth Job serve God for nought?" Certainly not; no man ever did or shall. Our earthly masters reward efficient service; why should one expect the Giver "of every good and perfect gift" to do less? Indeed, "If any man's work abide which he hath built thereupon, he shall receive a reward," (1 Cor. 3:14). Only His reward will be an incorruptible crown.

INCORRUPTIBLE CROWN

"Now they do it (practice strict discipline) to obtain a corruptible crown, but we an incorruptible" (1 Cor. 9:25). The "incorruptible crown" is a figure which symbolizes the reward which God will give for the approved Christian life and service. In this connection other crowns are spoken of in Scripture. James speaks of the "crown of life" which will be given to them who have been *tried* and *approved*, and who *love Him*: "Blessed is the man that endureth temptation, for when he hath been approved he shall receive the crown of life, which the Lord hath promised to them that love Him" (R. V., 1:12). Peter points to the "Crown of Glory," a reward for those who feed the flock of Christ with the food which God has provided in His Word: "And when the chief Shepherd shall appear, ye shall receive a crown of glory that fadeth not away" (1 Pet. 5:2-4).

Paul refers to two crowns. He speaks of the "crown of righteousness" which will be bestowed upon those who "love His appearing," who actually yearn for the Lord to return: "Henceforth there is laid up for me a crown of righteousness, which the Lord, the righteous judge, shall give me at that day: and not to me only, but unto all them also that love His appearing" (2 Tim. 4:8). And the "crown of rejoicing" is spoken of as the reward for soul-winning: "For what is our hope, or joy, or crown of rejoicing? Are not even ye in the presence of our Lord Jesus Christ at His coming?" (1 Thess. 2:19).

What do all the crowns signify?

The word "crown" in the Old Testament is a translation of five different Hebrew words, and in the New Testament it is a translation of two Greek words. The two Greek words are *diadema* and *stephanos*. They are both translated in our New Testament by the same word "crown" but their usage is different. *W. E. Raffety*, in the *International Standard Bible Encyclope-*

dia, summarized the uses of the crowns throughout the whole Bible as follows: "There are five uses of the crown as seen in the Scripture references studied, viz. decoration, consecration, coronation, exaltation, and remuneration." Coming back to the two Greek words, *diadema* and *stephanos*, for crown, we find that *diadema*, translated in the revised versions more accurately 'diadem,' is symbolic of sovereignty and power, and is used exclusively for denoting honor and exaltation. *Stephanos* is different in appearance and not so limited in its usage. It is a garland or wreath twisted out of leaves, pine-shoots, or olive branches, or even an assorted growth of the field. A garland weaved this way made the symbol more noticeable, more intricate, and more meaningful than if it were wreathed out of plain fillet, such as gold. Figuratively this crown (*Stephanos*) is used in Scripture largely in the realm of remuneration, as a reward for the approved Christian life and service."

The Scripture passages quoted above, which speak of the different crowns, all carry the use of this word *Stephanos*. The Apostles visualized the persistent, faithful believer at the end of his hard-won race rewarded accordingly with the significant garland, the *stephanos* of rejoicing (2 Thess. 2:19), the *stephanos* of righteousness (2 Tim. 4:8), the *stephanos* of glory (1 Pet. 5:4), the *stephanos* of life (Jas. 1:12).

It is hardly to be supposed that these several crowns symbolize for the victor-believers rewards in heaven in the form of separate be-jeweled objects which they may proudly carry around in a suitcase or prominently display on a what-not shelf in their mansions. We must look for their meaning elsewhere. The rewards will be more innately a part of the victors. He who has blessed all believers with innumerable spiritual blessings in heavenly places. He who is Himself infinite and eternal will surely make His consummate rewards to be such as will perpetually charm and delight the victor's whole being.

In the incident of the four and twenty elders casting their crowns at Jesus' feet we find illumination for the meaning of the crowns. "The four and twenty elders fall down before Him that sat on the throne, and worship Him that liveth for ever and ever, and cast their crowns before the throne, saying, Thou art worthy, O Lord, to receive glory and honour and power" (Rev. 4:10,11). These "four and twenty elders" represent the company of the redeemed in Heaven. They bear all the characteristics of the glorified Church: They are clothed in white; they worship the Lamb; they have been redeemed by the blood; they are round about the throne; they are crowned with glory and honor; they are kings and priests unto God; they hope to reign (Rev. 5:8-10).

Now notice: These elders cast their crowns at Christ's feet, saying, "Thou art worthy to receive *glory, and honour, and power.*" Then it is obvious that these crowns are symbolic of "glory, honour, and power." The redeemed ones are conscious of the fact that whatever they wrought that withstood the "fire" was done only in the strength of Christ. So they glorify Him, lay the crowns at His feet, saying, "Thou art worthy."

These crowns suggest to our dim powers of comprehension a life of indescribable blessedness in heaven—a life of "triumphant repose," of "festal enjoyment," of abundant rejoicing, of intensified capacities, of enriched companionship. The crown of "life," the crown of "glory," the crown of "rejoicing," the crown of "righteousness"—these together make up the "prize of the high calling of God in Christ Jesus our Lord."

Speaking of the various crowns and in attempting to combine their meaning and solidify them into one, *Alexander Maclaren* ventured the interpretation that the various "epithets describe the material, so to speak, of which the wreath is composed. The everlasting flower of life, the radiant blossoms of glory, the white flower of righteousness; these are its components." All these are the meaningful "components" of the "INCORRUPTIBLE CROWN."

Let us look a moment at these components of the "incorruptible crown." Here is the crown of "life." It is more than just life eternal. Every believer will have that. The crown of "life" is given for faithfulness to God in time of testing, because of whole-hearted love for Himself (Rev. 2:10), much time spent with Him alone, building "gold." This means endowment of life in heaven with more intense powers of spiritual life and consciousness. Their energies will be more buoyant, more elastic, and the outlets for their activities increased manifold.

The crown of "glory" suggests new inlets for the celestial glory and beauty. This crown is given for sincere fellowship with other believers—building "silver"—in ministering faithfully to them the spiritual food (1 Pet. 5:1-4). Now the diligent servant of God is made to drink deeply into the sacred delicacies of the blest. His whole being is enriched with a "lustrousness of character imparted by radiation and reflection from the central light of the glory of God."

And the crown of "rejoicing" is given to those whose wisdom is "more precious than rubies" because they won souls to the Lord Jesus Christ (1 Thess. 2:19; Phil. 4:1). No powers will be dull and dead. Every faculty will thrill with the joy of the Lord. These victors shall be made to blaze out in heavenly glory as the sun, and to shine forever and ever as the stars.

The crown of "righteousness" is given for "loving His appearing," sincerely desiring the wonderful Savior to come back, even as He has faithfully promised that He will (2 Tim. 4:8). We have before stated that these crowns do not depict external dignities, but rather they are spiritual dignities which adorn the soul. "Festal gladness," "calm repose," "flashing glory," solid rejoicing, and all fullness of life are not yet all the components of the incorruptible crown. There is this more, the crown of "righteousness," which, as Maclaren suggests, is "investiture with all purity . . . the very climax and culmination of the other hopes, declaring that absolute, stainless, infallible righteousness which one day" shall dignify and adorn the immortal lives of those who will attain. "They shall all walk with me in white."

These are the sprigs and the petals wreathed into the "incorruptible crown" by the fingers of the omniscient God, and across it His omnipotent hand has stamped the "signature of perpetuity." Indeed, a worthy "prize" for mortals whose blessed privilege and ample reward in itself was to suffer and to toil and to wait in the strength which He Himself supplied. The INCORRUPTIBLE CROWN! "It is twined of amaranth, ever blossoming into new beauty and never fading."

Somebody's bit of research shows that the *oldest* crown in the world is the iron crown of the Lombards now worn by the king of Italy. The *most famous* crown in the world is the crown of *Charlemagne*, which was worn by the Spanish kings. The *most beautiful* crown that ever adorned the brow of a ruler was that of *Robert Bruce*, made of the jewels of the Scottish ladies. The *richest* crown in the world is the crown of England, containing the famous "Kohinoor" stone and many other priceless gems.

But all these crowns are earthly and will pass away as the flower of the field.

There is one more crown that was made on earth. But it is *older* than the iron crown of the Lombards, *more beautiful* than the crown of Bruce, *more famous* than that of Charlemagne, *richer* than the crown of England. It is the *crown of thorns* that was placed upon the Savior's brow. It was platted by His enemies, and pressed upon His sacred head in hateful mockery. It pierced His brow and made blood freely flow down His cheeks. That crown has abiding reality. It will never fade. Redeemed ones shall ever behold it as a heavenly radiance about His head.

The "incorruptible crown" which God bestows upon those who have run the race of their Christian pilgrimage successfully is closely patterned after that crown of the Savior. They who "have fellowship in His sufferings," they who joyfully follow Him whithersoever He leads—stepping in blood-prints—they shall receive His approval and be crowned. "If we suffer [with Him], we shall also reign with Him" (2 Tim. 2:12).

All other crowns, all other rewards, all other prizes will pale into utter insignificance, and in a moment pass forever out of remembrance when the Supreme Judge of all the universe comes forth with the crowns incorruptible.

Transported into His glorious presence, we shall behold it all. God's prizes, the hope of millenniums, are about to be bestowed. They are not brilliant ribbons or medals of brass, or silver, or gold, but kingdoms of heavenly delight, mansions on the eternal hills, dominions of unfading power, empires of unending love, continents of everlasting light, oceans of billowing joy.

History records the great day when *Aurelian*, the Roman Emperor, came back from his victories. "In the front of the procession were wild beasts from all lands, 1600 gladiators richly clad, wagonloads of crowns presented by conquered cities; among the captives, Syrians, Egyptians, Goths, Vandals, Sarmatians, Franks; and Zenobia, the beautiful captive queen, on foot in chains of gold that a slave had to help her carry, and jewels under the weight of which she almost fainted. And then came the chariot of Aurelian, drawn by four elephants in gorgeous caparison and followed by the Roman Senate and the Roman army; and from dawn till dark the procession was passing. Rome in all her history never saw anything more magnificent."

But how much greater the day when our conqueror, Jesus, shall ride under the triumphant arches in heaven, His voluntary captives not on foot, but in brilliant chariots, all the redeemed of earth in procession, the armies celestial on white horses, rumbling artillery of thunderbolts, an innumerable company in line, centuries in line, saintly, cherubic, seraphic, archangelic splendors in line, and Christ, ordained by God to be

Judge, now seated on one great rolling hosanna, made out of all hallelujahs of all ages, shall cry "Halt" to the procession. All the redeemed shall gather at the Judgment Seat of Christ, and not forgetting even the humblest in all the reach of His omnipresence, He shall rise and then and there proceed, amid all ecstasy such as neither mortal nor immortal ever imagined, to divide the spoil. He had said, "Behold, I come quickly; and my reward is with me, to give every man according as his work shall be" (Rev. 22:12). And the watching victorious Church of Christ replies, "Even so, come, Lord Jesus" (Rev. 22:20).

Exceeding Great Reward

But our greatest reward will be to see face to face Him whom we have followed so long by faith, whom we have dearly loved, though without seeing Him; and to hear Him say, "I am thy shield and thy exceeding great reward."

"After these things the word of the Lord came unto Abram in a vision, saying, Fear not, Abram: I am thy shield and thy exceeding great reward" (Gen. 15:1). "After these things"— the reference is to the events of chapter 14, where it is recorded that Abram defeated an alliance of Asiatic kings and delivered thereby among others his nephew Lot and the kings of Sodom and Gomorrah, and also much goods. The king of Sodom offered to give Abram much booty, but the devoted man of faith refused to be enriched by a Sodomite, saying that his expectation and his reward were from the "most high God, the possessor of heaven and earth" (Gen. 14:22, 23). Abram was willing to wait for the recognition and applause of his God whom he fully trusted and whom he sought to glorify. Through faith in God, Abram turned down the spoil of Sodom and Gomorrah. God would not allow such a faithful heart to be a loser; so "after these things" God seeks him out, encourages him—"Fear not"— and bespeaks his true reward: "I am thy shield and thy exceeding great reward."

How wonderful! God was indeed a shield for this man, just

as He is to every trusting child of God today. Our great Savior is the believer's rest, the believer's peace, and the believer's security. No dart of the enemy can ever penetrate the shield of the Almighty. He is our Sure Foundation, or Tried Foundation, our Abiding Foundation. God made to Abram the observation that He was his shield. God also desires *us* to remember that it is in His wonderful redemption through the Lord Jesus Christ that He has brought us safe thus far, that through Him, the chief Corner Stone, God has kept us, and through Him we shall be presented "faultless before the presence of His glory with exceeding joy" (Jude 24).

Now notice please. It is the God who hath been our "shield" all through the pilgrimage, who now saith to His own, "I am thy exceeding great reward." He Himself would be His servant's greatest reward. Somebody once borrowed Moody's Bible, and when it came back it had this written on the fly leaf:

The light of heaven is the face of Jesus
The joy of heaven is the presence of Jesus
The melody of heaven is the name of Jesus
The harmony of heaven is the praise of Jesus
The theme of heaven is the work of Jesus
The employment of heaven is the service of Jesus
The duration of heaven is the eternity of Jesus
The fullness of heaven is Jesus Himself.

The privileged Apostles who saw Christ transfigured on the Mount, it so happened in the course of the fellowship, that they saw no one save "Jesus only," even so in heaven Christ will be the preeminent one.

Let me ask you: When that father, or that son, or that husband came home from across the wide seas whence he had gone in service of country, what was it that you were looking forward to most in connection with his return? Was it the stories of travel and heroism that he would have to tell? Was it the trinkets and antiques and valuables that he would bring?

Oh, no, it was the insuperable joy of seeing again his face. You thought of each other, wrote to each other, prayed for each other, longed for each other. But it is quite painful being absent from the one so loved. And now again the joy of his presence!

When the Battle of Britain was being fought out in the skies over that country, one night a throng of people rushed into a large Air Raid Shelter. Presently a bomb exploded close by. Screams, faintings, and panic ensued. Some began to run out with or without their children. Others were madly running around and crying hysterically. A little old woman rose to some elevation and began to quieten them down. She was quite ordinary looking. Her husband died in World War I. Her son was at this time in the Royal Air Force. Tried and tested herself, she was now convincing and eloquent as she pleaded with them to be calm: "Stop running out. It's worse out there. Why be afraid? We have committed our case to God. Our confidence is in Him. We are English women," etc., etc. There was a stillness. Women came back and hugged their children. Someone lighted a candle. The woman, who had probably never before made a speech in her life, waxed eloquent for quite a while pouring out her heart to them. Then there were prayers.

A few days later, on February 14, 1941, *King George VI* searched out this poor wash woman. He pinned a medal on her calico dress, shook her hand, looked her in the face, and said, "All of Britain is proud of you."

Remarkable! I would suggest an observation that you have, no doubt, already noted. The poor woman's greatest reward was not the medal, but the approval of her honored Monarch, who sought her out, and whom she saw face to face. This was her "exceeding great reward."

Even so, even so, our hearts do sigh and long for Him whom we have loved so long, and whose face we have not seen. It is wonderful to believe in Him, to walk with Him by faith, to enjoy the presence and the comfort of the Holy Spirit who whispers to us sweet things concerning the Savior. We love serving Him. We delight in the extended opportunity of leading souls to Him. Truly, for us "to live is Christ." We are occupied with Him night and day. But, oh, how we do long to behold Him face to face, and we cry out, "Make no tarrying, Lord." His coming will end all conflicts forever. His presence will banish all shadows.

We can well understand why the saintly *Samuel Rutherford*, when he was nearing the end of earth's pilgrimage, was so gloriously excited at the prospect of seeing Christ that those about him felt obligated to counsel him to moderate his ecstasy. The rich effects of that glorious expectancy should pervade all our days. Meditation upon the prospect of seeing Christ face to face and of living forever with Him will fill life with quiet and fruitful amazement.

Not only shall we see Him face to face, "but we know that, when He shall appear, we shall be like Him; for we shall see Him as He is" (1 Jn. 3:2). Then it is that the Lord "shall change our vile body, that it may be fashioned like unto His glorious body" (Phil 3:21). Like the Psalmist of old, every ardent disciple of Christ in our uncertain times looks up and says, "As for me, I will behold Thy face in righteousness: I shall be satisfied, when I awake, with Thy likeness" (Psa. 17:15).

"After these things!" Yes, after the "things" of our earthly sojourn. So much of what consumes our energies and our time is just "things." "After these things the word of the Lord came unto _____ (you might put your name there), saying, Fear not, I am thy shield and thy exceeding great reward!"

The night is far spent. The day is at hand. Let us look up as the consummation of our redemption is drawing nigh.

Suddenly they cry, "HE COMES!" Yes, in a moment, in a twinkling of an eye. The angel blows one loud resurrectionary blast. The graves of those who died in Christ are opened, and millions of departed spirits are reclothing themselves in forms now radiant for ascension. Believers living then on earth are translated into immortality in a moment and instantly rising to meet the Lord in the air. Upward and away! Up, up! Forward, ye ranks of God Almighty! Lift up your heads, ye everlasting gates, and let the conquerors come in!

Every eye is turned on Him! Every heart is beating fast and craving inexpressibly His approval. He has the rewards with Him, the immortal prize, the incorruptible crown. Perfect stillness—behold the FIRE. "Wood, hay, stubble" consumed, but "gold, silver, precious stones" abide. Look! Look! He is bestowing the incorruptible crowns!! Oh, what joy! Oh! What blessedness!

But the insuperable joy and crown and EXCEEDING GREAT REWARD shall be when the Altogether Lovely and Adorable Lord looks you in the face, and before all the heavenly hosts He says to you, "Well done, thou good and faithful servant. God the Father, God the Son, God the Holy Spirit, all the angelic powers, all the redeemed hosts, all the General Assembly of heaven are proud of you, enter thou into the joy of the Lord." Oh, God, can it be that my eyes are blind to eternity! Oh, God, help me!

> A moment more, and I may be
> Caught up in glory, Lord with Thee;
> And raptured sight! Thy face to see
> Forevermore!
> —*L. S. Chafer*

He shall then present us to the Father with exceeding joy, and say to us, like the king of old said to the man of God, "Come home with me and refresh thyself" (1 Kings 13:7). Living with Him! Reigning with Him! A New Heaven! A New Earth! Roll on, eternity, roll on!